TEXAS TRIVIA

EVERYTHING Y'ALL NEED TO KNOW
ABOUT THE LONE STAR STATE

BILL CANNON

Revised by Courtney Oppel

LONE
STAR
BOOKS

Guilford, Connecticut
Helena, Montana

LONE STAR BOOKS

An imprint of The Rowman & Littlefield Publishing Group, Inc.
4501 Forbes Blvd., Ste. 200
Lanham, MD 20706
www.rowman.com
A registered trademark of The Rowman & Littlefield Publishing Group, Inc.

Distributed by NATIONAL BOOK NETWORK

British Library Cataloguing in Publication Information available

Library of Congress Cataloging-in-Publication Data

ISBN 978-1-4930-3241-9 (paperback)
ISBN 978-1-4930-3242-6 (e-book)

∞™ The paper used in this publication meets the minimum requirements of American National Standard for Information Sciences—Permanence of Paper for Printed Library Materials, ANSI/NISO Z39.48-1992.

Printed in the United States of America

CONTENTS

Annexation of Texas – Fifty Cent Act – Car-Barn
Convention – The Five States of Texas? – Missouri Capital
in Texas – Capitol Coup – Semicolon Court – The Capitol
Syndicate – Bonham's "Mr. Speaker," Sam Rayburn – John
Nance "Cactus Jack" Garner – Jim Ferguson – Miriam A.
"Ma" Ferguson – W. Lee "Pappy" O'Daniel – Landslide
Lyndon – Monumental Name Ban – Will Travel for Sugar –
Chrysler's Dodge Texan – The Wet Town That Dried Up

Gone to Texas – The Yellow Rose of Texas – Siesta Theory –
Hazardous Occupation – Juneteenth – "The Eyes of Texas"
Prank – Texas A&M's Twelfth Man – Texas-Leaguer – A
Prickly Topic – State Fish – Inflated Currency – Redbacks
– Civil War Stamps – The Great Pearl Rush – Salt Domes –
Texas-Size Steak Challenge – Paris's Eiffel Tower Receives
Traditional Texas Topping – Jesus in Cowboy Boots
– Rattlesnakes and Wasps – "One Riot–One Ranger" –
Texas's Unkindest Insult – Hidden Secrets of the "Ugly Old
Goddess" of Austin – Shelby County Courthouse's Trap Door
– "Pecosin'" a Feared Word – The Jackass Mail – Rickshaws
under Texas Skies

First Surgery – First Thanksgiving – Nacagdoches, Site of
First Christmas in Texas – José de Escandón – Anaqua – San
Jacinto Flag – First Baptist Church in Texas – Old News –
The Legend of the First Bowie Knife – Death by the Rope
in Dallas – First Flight – Texas's First Civil Rights March
– First Oil Well – The First Bridge Across the Brazos –
Oldest Public School – Telephones – "Old Tige" – First Auto
Trip – The Great Storm of 1900 – Public Demonstration
of Airplane – First Alamo Movie – The Coolest Buildings
– Bowie County's Largest Baby – New London School

INTRODUCTION

TWENTY YEARS AGO, WHEN THE LATE AUTHOR BILL CANNON first put together two volumes of Texas trivia, he brought to light some of the more interesting stories from the Lone Star State that had fallen between the cracks of recorded history. In the years since, other have taken up the gauntlet to seek out the truth of these fascinating gems hidden in the treasure troves we call libraries, museums, and past generations' memories.

Thanks to the marvel of the Internet, it's easy to access reliable sources for updated information and simply to get some "facts" straightened out. In the process, several entries from the original volumes didn't make the cut: One county (Winkler) that twenty years ago was recorded to be the second-to-least populated county in the state has since experienced (relatively) explosive growth, an iconic tree has exhaled its last oxygen, businesses have

changed hands or closed, and facts have arisen to debunk certain long-standing legends as nothing but fodder for campfire stories (which is probably how they got started). Nevertheless, some accounts continue to fascinate us as we dig deeper. The origins of the mysterious rock wall in Rockwall County continue to spark debates among geologists and archaeologists—and the more they discover about it, the more questions arise. Although a marker in Round Rock declares that town to be the final resting place of outlaw Sam Bass, old-timers insisted he made it all the way to Grapevine before succumbing to fatal bullet wounds and that he was buried surreptitiously near their family plot. And who knew that the all-American sandwich that has taken the world by storm and driven fast-food enterprises into international fame and fortune—the humble hamburger—was invented by a Texan? It was, wasn't it?

If, in reading these lesser-known facts about this amazing state's people, places, and events, you're inspired to do some of your own digging, this updated edition of *Texas Trivia* will have served a noble purpose—and you'll be just a little bit smarter than your average Texan.

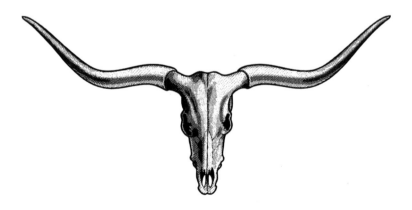

TRUTH IS STRANGER
THAN FICTION

TRIVIA IS DESCRIBED IN *MERRIAM-WEBSTER'S COLLEGIATE DICTIO-nary* as "unimportant matters; trivial facts or details." Whether one thinks of Texas simply as a land mass or as the Utopia spoken of by its inhabitants as "having the biggest and best of everything known to man," it is difficult to say anything is "trivial" about it. This is the state that was once a republic, a state whose history almost explodes from the pages of history books, a state that boasts a population whose culture is molded from the hundreds of diverse cultures that settled and developed it and elevated it to the preeminence it enjoys among people all over the world today. The evolution of Texas has produced a wealth of little-known facts that are not only informative but also interesting and humorous. The reader is sure to find some details that prove the old adage "Truth is stranger than fiction," but take into consideration these bits of trivia are from a state where people believe that boasting isn't bragging if it's true!

CADILLAC RANCH
One of the best-known examples of Texas eccentricity is the field of Cadillacs outside Amarillo. The row of ten different-year model Caddies was "planted" hood-first in the ground by city inhabitant (and eccentric millionaire) Stanley Marsh, simply to display the change in tail-fin design between 1948 and 1964. Over the years,

vandals have taken off with various car parts—prompting the need to weld the remaining parts onto the cars—and what's left is covered with layers of graffiti.

BURY THE HATCHET . . . AND TOMAHAWK . . . AND HORSE

Though it is said that the phrase "to bury the hatchet" (let bygones be bygones) originated with the New England Indians, who sealed a peace treaty by ceremoniously burying an ax, their principal weapon of war, apparently this ceremony was also practiced in Texas. When early settlers and Indians in Spanish missions were terrorized by hostile Indians, efforts to make peace sometimes resulted in an unusual treaty. According to historians, a ceremony was held in which the Indians buried a live horse as well as a tomahawk and other implements of war.

CANE PROXY

Have you ever heard of a town being ruled by a walking cane? Back in Texas's infancy, the top city official or mayor was called by the Spanish name for town leader: alcalde. As a sign of office, the alcalde carried a silver-headed cane, and when he couldn't appear in person, he could be represented by sending his cane!

CONFORM OR STAY HOME!

Early Texas settlers had many adjustments to make if they seriously considered taking advantage of land opportunities in the new frontier of Texas. Not only did they face the formidable prospects of bringing the hostile land into submission, they had to be ready to defend themselves against equally hostile Indians who were as eager to prevent the loss of their hunting lands as the settlers were of gaining land for farming and ranching.

But perhaps the most disturbing changes for many of them were imposed upon them by the Mexican government. In order to settle in Texas, the settlers had to become Mexican citizens and had to be Catholic. We know that Alamo hero Jim Bowie became a Mexican citizen in 1830. He was not only a Mexican citizen but was married to a Mexican when he fought against the Mexicans at the Alamo!

Latin in Latium

A region composed of five communities—Millheim in Austin County, Latium in Washington County, Sisterdale and Tusculum in Kendall County, and Bettina in Llano County—was settled in the 1840s by highly educated Germans. Literature seemed to be the catalyst that bonded the settlements, and it is written that regular debates were held in Latin. Incidentally, Latium was the name of the Latin-speaking region in Italy that included Rome.

German Ingenuity

The Kendall County town of Comfort was the setting of an unusual event that occurred about two years after its founding. The town was founded by German settlers from New Braunfels in 1854. The town was in possession of a cannon, which was to be fired to alert the townspeople in the event of an emergency, such as an Indian attack or fire. However, the cannon became useful in solving another serious if somewhat unorthodox emergency, according to local historian Greg Krauter.

Mr. Krauter told us that in preparation for Comfort's celebration of the Fourth of July, a wagonload of beer had been ordered from the Menger Brewery in San Antonio. The wagon, however, arrived two days early, and with the beer not being pasteurized and there being no cold storage in those days, the cannon was fired to draw the citizens into town and alert them to what for Germans would be a catastrophe: the loss of a wagon of beer!

Mr. Krauter said there was a minor uprising of the citizens because, by definition, the cannon shot was a false alarm. When faced with the situation, the Germans rose to the occasion and solved the problem in a most logical way: They celebrated Fourth of July on the second of July and drank the beer before it could spoil!

SHACKELFORD COUNTY'S ALPHABET JAIL

Albany, Texas, county seat of Shackelford County, is the home of a Texas county jail with two special attractions to visitors—not to those sent there by judicial decree but to those of us who ferret out unique Texas attractions. According to historical records, verified by jail historian Diana Nail, outlaw and occasional lawman John Selman escaped from the jail in the late 1870s. Selman found his way to El Paso, where he earned a notch on his gun as well as a special place in Texas history. He is given credit as being the gunslinger that killed badman-turned-lawyer John Wesley Hardin.

The Albany jail has, it should be noted, one additional claim to fame. It was given the name "Alphabet Jail." It was so named because when it was built in 1878, the county suffered from a lack of funds and the stone masons carved their initials into each stone they cut to be insured they would be paid for their work. Ms. Nail advised us that the initials can be seen both inside and outside the jail. This example of piecework payment, strange as it is, is true!

ONE-STUDENT SCHOOLHOUSE

Effie Thomas, who was born in the 1890s, told of her pioneer teaching days in the Panhandle near the famous Goodnight Ranch. She related how an area rancher named Cobel had an accredited school built on his ranch and got state aid to hire a teacher, who, incidentally, boarded at the Cobel home. She taught the school's only pupil, Cobel's daughter, who couldn't attend existing schools because of the distance.

JUDGE ROY BEAN RENDERS TKO TO PRIZEFIGHT LAW

Charles Allen Culberson, the twenty-first governor of the state of Texas, served from January 15, 1895, to January 17, 1899. In 1895 Culberson convened the legislature to prohibit prizefighting in Texas after plans had been made for the James "Gentleman Jim" Corbett–Bob Fitzsimmons match to be held in Dallas before a crowd of fifty-three thousand. He called the match "an act of public barbarism." A court had held that prizefighting did not violate the law; the legislative bill was passed prohibiting prizefighting in Texas.

But the governor was to learn that the sparring had just begun. The Fitzsimmons-Corbett match was moved to Carson City, Nevada, where Corbett was defeated. Culberson later asked the Rangers to keep the Fitzsimmons–Peter Maher fight from being held in Texas.

Judge Roy Bean, known as "the Law West of the Pecos," used his personal style of fancy footwork to circumvent the law the following year when he staged the Fitzsimmons-Maher heavy-weight championship fight in a ring built on a sandbar in the bed of the Rio Grande just below Langtry on February 21, 1896. The bout had been forbidden in Texas, New Mexico, and Arizona. By building his ring across the river in Mexican territory, Bean out-witted the Rangers who had been dispatched to stop him.

The Great Crash at Crush

Though Texas has a legendary reputation for bragging and spec-tacular stories, the crash near Crush seems almost too much even for the natives to believe. But on September 15, 1896, George Crush, a passenger agent for Missouri, Kansas & Texas Railroad, engineered the publicity stunt of all time when he carried out his idea of having two M.K. & T. steam locomotives run at each other at 90 mph. He was hoping the event would attract enough passen-gers on special trains to pay for it. Some fifty thousand spectators arrived on thirty special trains and assembled in a field between West and Waco to see the great crash, which was catastrophic if not spectacular. Two people were killed and many injured when the two boilers exploded. The railroad settled all claims by the injured as quickly as they were presented. Amazingly, this stunt gained popularity and was used nearly one hundred times—largely at state fairs and with safeguards in place—but died out as a symbol of conspicuous consumption during the Great Depression.

Courthouse Moved by Cowboys

A 1903 election moved the county seat of Hartley County from Hartley to Channing, which was the headquarters of the famed XIT Ranch. The Panhandle county was the scene of an ahead-of-its-time transportation feat: Enterprising cowboys from the XIT put the old frame courthouse on wheels and towed it behind their horses to the new county seat. The old courthouse was trans-formed into a hotel when a new brick courthouse was constructed in 1906.

St. Elmo's Fire in Texas

Early Texas trail drivers, while herding the massive herds of Texas cattle over the historic trails of Texas, were sometimes treated, especially during storms, to a bizarre phenomenon in which eerie luminous flashes of yellow-green tongues of lightning-like fire arced from the horns of one steer to the horns of a nearby steer. Often this early-day "laser show" continued until the entire herd was bathed in an incandescent glow. This phenomenon, although a mystery to the cowpokes of old, is today associated with ships' masts and aircraft. It is technically known as St. Elmo's Fire.

Taft's Train "Willed" to Stop

According to the *Wills Point Chronicle* of October 28, 1909, Robert McLeod of VanZandt County, by cutting a cotton cord, caused a president of the United States to make an unscheduled speech. This enabled hundreds of Texans for the first time in their lives to see and hear the president of the United States. On October 24, 1909, residents of Wills Point and the territory for miles around came to town to see William Howard Taft as he stopped there on his tour of Texas. The president's private car was attached to the regular ten o'clock Texas and Pacific "Cannon Ball," which was a regular train through town. Even more important, the chief executive had promised to greet the people of the town at the station.

When it was decided to make a "special" of the train, the railroad gave orders cutting out all the stops along the way. This was not learned in Wills Point until a large crowd had gathered in hopes of seeing and hearing the president. There was a semaphore atop the station that signaled the engineers whether to stop or continue through town, and it was in the vertical (go) position. A bystander who was an engineer was overheard saying, "It would be too bad if someone cut the cord which allows the semaphore to drop from the vertical position to the horizontal position." A plucky Bob McLeod of Van Zandt heard him and, showing no fear of railroad officials, climbed atop the station and, as the train pulled into the yards, cut the cotton cord. This allowed the signal to drop to the "stop" position; the engineer promptly stopped the train, and the president came forth and made a brief speech. Effie Thomas, who was born in Wills Point, said that when Taft asked, "What town is this?" and someone responded, "Wills Point," the president replied, "It sure is a town with a will, all right!"

"Bat Cave" Jail

The dungeon-like jail of Fort Davis, onetime county seat of Presidio County, was underneath the adobe court house. Known as the "bat cave," its entrance was a trap door and ladder in the floor of the sheriff's office. According to the minutes of the Commissioner's Court, it was outfitted with five iron cages and a scaffold. Referring to the move to the new county seat, the court minutes indicate that "all records, books, and furniture except five iron cages and a scaffold in the jail have been moved to Marfa." The old "bat cave" courthouse was replaced on the same site with a modern concrete and stone structure in 1911.

Everything but the Kitchen (Not Even a Sink)

There is no longer any written documentation, but a descendent of one of the parties involved tells of a huge blunder in the design of the elegant Galvez Hotel on Galveston Island, long a playground for socialites, politicos, and others of society's "upper crust." In all its grandeur, the Galvez, which opened in 1911, was designed

with no provisions for a kitchen. Those connected with its construction claim that after bids had been let, it was discovered that the plans did not include a kitchen, so one was built in a separate building to "cover up" the error. The hotel where band leader Phil Harris and Alice Fay were married and where President Franklin D. Roosevelt stayed when he went deep-sea fishing in the Gulf nevertheless did much to breathe life into a sagging island economy, attached kitchen or no.

CUERO'S "TURKEY TROT"

Although it may sound like one, this DeWitt County city's unusual claim to fame is no dance but a parade of sorts. Each year since 1912 turkey buyers have driven a flock of the birds through Cuero to herald the opening of the fall market season. After buying turkeys from outlying farms, buyers drive the gobblers into Cuero. In 1962, Cuero began celebrating TurkeyFest, a three-day event in October that still includes the "Gobbler Gallop" turkey roundup, along with a carnival, a 5K "Turkey Trot" race (for people), and other family-friendly activities. This ritual underscores this South Texas county's claim to being "the turkey capital of the world."

THE CURSE ON THE COURTHOUSE CLOCK

Legend says that the clock in the county courthouse in Gonzales is cursed. In 1921, though he claimed innocence, Albert Howard was executed in Gonzales. It is said that while he waited to be hanged, he watched the clock on the courthouse as it ticked away his last hours. Howard swore that his innocence would be demonstrated by the clock, which would never keep correct time again. Since his hanging, the four faces of the clock have never kept the same time despite attempts to repair it.

CHARLES LINDBERGH'S CRASH

Prior to his transatlantic flight between New York City and Paris, Charles Lindbergh was scheduled to report as a flying cadet at

Brooks Field in San Antonio on March 15, 1924. In the interim from February to mid-March, he and some others did some flying, and on several occasions Lindbergh's plane crashed, according to a biographer. On one occasion he and a friend, running low on gas, made a forced landing near the headwaters of the Neuces River. The pasture was so small that the plane couldn't take off again with both of them, so Lindbergh went up alone and landed again in the town square at Camp Wood in Real County. He attempted to take off from a street, and though he tried to avoid utility poles and wires, his wing tip clipped a pole and his plane spun around into a hardware store. The owner refused payment for damages, saying the publicity was worth more than the cost of repairing the wall. Three years later an improved Lindbergh made his historical solo transatlantic flight.

VINTAGE NEWS IN NORTH TEXAS

One sure way to revisit history is by reading the newspapers of yesteryear. Thanks to the Grapevine Heritage Foundation, we were able to scan a decades-old edition of that city's *Grapevine Sun*, which enabled us to reach back in time and glean a few stories that were newsworthy at the time. In some cases we found the news was not so different from today's. We found some that today we find almost laughable, while others were most horrific! We offer the following as examples of yesterday's noteworthy news.

The biggest headline grabber in the Easter Sunday, April 1, 1934, edition of the *Grapevine Sun* involved the infamous Barrow gang. This story may well be burned in the memory of some of us today! The headlines read, "BONNIE AND CLYDE MURDER LOCAL POLICEMEN." That's right, policemen, plural! The story reminds us how "three motorcycle policemen were patrolling on Highway 114 west out of Grapevine. One officer, twenty-four-year-old H. D. Murphy, was on his first day of official patrol duty. He was scheduled to be married in a few days to his twenty-year-old fiancée in Alto, Texas." The officers saw a car parked on a side road. One officer rode ahead and the other two tagged behind. The first officer later noticed that the other two were not behind him. He returned and found them lying dead in the road. The two had decided to investigate. A farmer sitting on his front porch was able to give an account as to what happened:

The two stopped, dismounted, and with guns in holsters walked towards the parked car. When they got within twenty-five feet of the car a man and woman stepped out of the vehicle, each firing shotguns. Both officers fell, mortally wounded. The farmer said the woman walked calmly over to one officer on the ground and shot him again. Then she and the man got into the car and drove off.

The farmer's eyewitness account linked Clyde Barrow and Bonnie Parker to the slayings.

Another headline from the police blotter, while not so dramatic, points out another item from days gone by: the simple headline "FILLING STATION ROBBED." Bearing the dateline "Grapevine, Feb. 21, 1935," the gist of the story is that during the commission of an armed robbery, which would be commonplace today, "the masked bandit took the cash from the cash register and gathered up the cigarettes and a slot machine from the counter, rushed to a waiting car and made off going west." We found it noteworthy that there was, at this time in Texas, "one-armed bandits" openly in service in some businesses.

Another headline in the old newspaper would be ludicrous today, especially with Grapevine's sitting on the threshold of one of the world's busiest airports. The headline reads, "NINE-YEAR PLANE." The brief item tells us that "Thelma Daniels got quite a start the other day. She was working in a field with her father when she heard a noise overhead. She looked up and saw an airplane for the very first time!" The item tells how she was so surprised she kept looking up. She was plowing with a one-row mule. She heard her father shout at her, "Get off that one row!"

Perhaps it is important for us to be able to look back every now and then and learn what was important to those who preceded us. In doing so we are reminded of those things that have slipped through our collective memories.

Bois d'Arc Streets

The bois d'arc tree, whose name means "wood of the bow," was named by French explorers moving southward who noticed that the tree was selected for bows by the Indians because of its strength and resiliency. Bois d'arc was also used in making wagons. Victor Doerle was an early Dallas blacksmith who constructed wagons using bois d'arc wood at his shop on Commerce Street between Houston and Record Streets.

Bois d'arc also helped lift Dallas out of the mud: According to local historians, the wood, cut into blocks, was used to pave Dallas streets in the 1880s. At that time the city accepted no responsibility for street paving, so the cost was borne by residents whose property abutted the street on both sides. The strong trees also served as fences between properties. These durable trees, planted as fences or property markers, are still quite common.

Streets Paved with Gold

During more prosperous times, the Texas Highway Department has proven that Texas really is "heaven on earth," as some of our streets are indeed paved with gold! Further proof is stated on a historical marker five miles south of Ringgold on US 81. The pavement on sections of US 81 and US 287 in Montague County actually contains gold. When the two highways were being paved in 1936, sand for the concrete was taken from a nearby pit. Seeing glints of gold in the sand, the owner of the pit had samples tested, but although the laboratory confirmed that it was gold, there was only about fifty-four cents' worth of gold per ton of ore, and it was very difficult to separate from the sand, making it not worth the expense. In all, sand containing about $250,000 worth of gold was mixed into the concrete for thirty-nine miles of the two highways.

THE *HINDENBURG* DISASTER

Had the *Hindenburg* been filled with Texas helium, one of the world's most infamous disasters might have been prevented. Unfortunately, this tragedy—and the resulting premature death of the dirigible transport industry—were the result of strict laws combined with nationalistic hubris.

The gigantic German airship burst into flames on May 6, 1937, as it prepared to moor at the Lakehurst Naval Air Station in New Jersey, killing thirty-five passengers and crew aboard and one crewman on the ground. Until then, more than a million miles had been safely logged by airship passengers, and a cooperative venture was in the works between the United States, Europe, and South America by American Zeppelin Transport Inc. to fly two nine-million-cubic-foot, helium-filled, American-built dirigibles across the Atlantic and to South America. But the fiery death of the *Hindenburg*, filled with highly flammable hydrogen gas, ended any plans for further use of airships for public transport.

Had helium been used in the *Hindenburg*, it might have been an entirely different story, but helium was found in only a handful of places—Amarillo, Texas, being one of them. It was rigidly protected under the Helium Act of 1927, which prevented the sale of this precious natural resource—surplus gas could only be leased to American citizens or corporations. Making the unfeasible even more impossible was the fierce, self-sufficient Nazi German pride. Germany never formally requested helium from the United States. The captain of the *Hindenburg* himself, Ernst Lehmann, was quoted as having said, "Even if we could get helium from America, we wouldn't ask for it." Lehmann was fatally burned in the crash.

JAPAN BOMBS TEXAS

In the spring of 1945 the war in Europe was nearing conclusion and more attention was turned to the war in the Pacific, thousands of miles away from the rural Texas farming communities of Woodson in Throckmorton County and Desdemona in Eastland County. Both were farming and ranching communities, and both had sent fathers and sons to war. The Japanese launched thousands of balloon bombs with incendiary devices attached in November of 1944, with hopes that they would ride the jet stream east into the United States and cause civilian casualties. Indeed, on March 23–24, 1945, Woodson and Desdemona were "bombed" by the Japanese, supposedly in retaliation for Jimmy Doolittle's raid on Tokyo in 1942. No damage was done, and there were no injuries. The bombs were discovered by school children and a ranch hand.

SUPER 'POSSUM

The common Texas opossum is unaffected by the bite of most poisonous snakes, including the copperhead, rattlesnake, and water moccasin. Only the coral snake is the opossum's kryptonite.

TEXAS STATE MAMMAL HAS STRANGE REPRODUCTION

The nine-banded armadillo, named Texas's state small mammal by the legislature, has a most unusual reproduction pattern. Each birth produces a litter of four, all of the same sex.

¿DE DÓNDE ES?

DID YOU EVER WONDER, "WHERE ON EARTH DID THAT NAME OR saying come from?" If you're a native who's lived in Texas your whole life, you've likely got a long list of such terms or names, and you assume you know what they mean. Or maybe you've heard so many different stories throughout the years that you've decided the truth is too hard to pin down. Regardless of whether you're a longtime resident, a visitor, or a recent transplant, here's a quick primer in Texanese.

TEXAS HOWDY

The word *Tejas*, from which comes the word Texas, is said to be the Spanish rendition of the greeting Spanish explorers received from the Hasinai (Caddoan) Indians and means friend or ally. In recognition of this translation, the state motto, "Friendship," was adopted by the Forty-First State Legislature in February of 1930.

YOU SAY GREEN GROW, I SAY GRINGO

Gringo, the Latin American slang word used to denote English-speaking foreigners, especially North Americans, originated during the Mexican-American War of 1846–1848. A popular soldier's song sung by Americans contained the phrase "Green grow the violets," which to the Mexicans who heard it sounded like "gringo" instead of "green grow." The term was thereafter associated with the "Norte Americanos."

How the Alamo Got Its Name

One famous landmark in Texas was named for the cottonwood tree. The Spanish mission Alamo was named for a grove of cottonwood trees nearby; *alamo* is the Spanish word for "cottonwood."

Original Barbecue

The origin of Texas barbecue is an interesting one, to say the least. "Barbecue" is a corruption of the Spanish word *barbacoa*, which was a Sunday breakfast that dates back to the Spanish *vaquero* (cowboy). During the early days of Texas, it was customary for a landowner to slaughter a cow at the end of the week. The landowner generally kept the carcass for himself and donated the head to the vaqueros. The vaqueros dug a pit and layered it with mesquite coals and rocks on the bottom, then wrapped the cow's head in wet burlap and lowered it into the coals. They covered the head with rocks and aromatic leaves or dirt and cactus. It was left to steam overnight and ready for a feast Sunday morning.

The XIT Ranch

Ranches and cattle brands have always been a fascination to Texans and non-Texans alike. The lore attached to some of the ranches and their brands are frequently reflective of the state's history. Such is the case with the XIT Ranch and its brand. (By the way, it's pronounced "X-I-T" and not "exit.") The ranch was established in 1885 as a piece of land totaling 3,050,000 acres given to the Chicago firm that built the state capitol building in Austin. This massive ranch covered all or at least most of ten counties in Texas. The designer of the XIT livestock brand says that the design was chosen because it would be difficult to alter; however, the brand gave rise to the generally accepted ranch name "Ten-In-Texas" (X standing for ten counties, IT for In Texas).

KING RANCH

Santa Gertrudis cattle, a distinctively Texas breed, were developed on the gigantic King Ranch in Texas by Robert Justus Kleberg. The breed was named for the Santa Gertrudis land grant from which the ranch was built. The King Ranch had its beginning in 1852, when Richard King purchased a Spanish land grant of seventy-five thousand acres in Nueces County on the Santa Gertrudis Creek. After King's death, his widow asked his lawyer, Kleberg, to manage the ranch. It was under Kleberg's management that the now famous breed of cattle was developed. Kleberg married King's daughter, Alice Gertrudis King. Kleberg's ranch, his cattle, and his wife's name originate from the same root.

FRYING PAN RANCH

The so-called Frying Pan Ranch was located in today's Potter County in the Panhandle. It was built as a model ranch to demonstrate the effectiveness of the newly marketed barbed wire. Its cattle brand was in the shape of a panhandle, and as a result, cowboys on the ranch renamed it "Frying Pan Ranch."

WINCHESTER QUARANTINE

The Winchester Quarantine had nothing to do with diseased firearms. It was in fact an "extra-legal device" used by Panhandle ranchers to staunch the northward movement of cattle that might spread the cattle tick. Charles Goodnight of the JA Ranch and

O. H. Nelson of the Shoe Bar posted guards along the forty-five-mile stretch between the ranches so that nesters moving north were required to go around the line or turn the cattle over to the watchmen until the first frost (and with it, the end of tick season). Because of the ready-loaded guns of the guards, the line was called the "Winchester Quarantine."

POINSETTIA

One of our best-loved Christmas symbols is named for a transplanted Texan. The poinsettia is named for Joel Poinsett, an amateur botanist originally from South Carolina. It's said that while Poinsett served as the first US minister to Mexico from 1825 to 1829, he took a liking to the showy flower while living in Texas. When he introduced the flower to Washington, DC, it was named after him.

THE OLD 300

A Dutchman of "questionable honesty" is the namesake for Bastrop County and was influential in obtaining land grants to attract some of the first Anglo settlers to Texas. Some believe that Baron de Bastrop, who was born in Holland, was a tax collector there and absconded with all the tax revenues. But here, Bastrop seems to have done well. He used all his influence with the Spanish governor of Texas to get him to listen to Moses Austin, father of Stephen F. Austin. Moses had approached the governor with plans to bring Anglo colonists to settle Texas, but the plan had been rejected and Austin was told to leave. De Bastrop was very influential with the governor and intervened for Austin. As a result, Austin was able to get land grants and to bring three hundred families into Texas. These first families went on to be known in history as "the old 300."

TWO BITS

We are familiar with the expressions "two bits, four bits, six bits" when speaking of American coinage, but does anyone really know what a bit is? Early Texans had to know: some posted rates for river ferries indicated the cost for transporting one small animal, such as a hog, was one bit. As coins were a rarity in early Texas, colonists used the Spanish silver dollar known as "pieces of eight." These were minted in Mexico City in 1535 and in the 1730s. The coin could actually be cut into eight pie-shaped pieces called "bits." Each bit was worth twelve and a half cents in US currency. When the United States coined the quarter, it was worth twenty-five cents, or two bits. The half dollar was worth four bits and so on. The word *peso* is actually an abbreviation for the phrase *peso del ocho,* meaning the weight of a piece of the eight.

CORDUROY ROADS

During the early days of oil discovery and development in Texas, drilling crews frequently found accessibility to their work hampered by seas of mud around the drilling rigs. According to Houston wildcatter Glenn McCarthy, at times the so-called roads were hip-deep in mud on a man and belly-deep on a horse or mule. When all vehicles were so mired, drilling crews would lay logs on the roads to travel on. These were referred to as "corduroy roads."

DAISY BRADFORD

Although the name Daisy Bradford might not be emphasized in Texas history classes, it is an important one in state history, especially to the people of East Texas. It was on Daisy Bradford's land that C. M. "Dad" Joiner drilled the Daisy Bradford #3 oil well, which was the gusher that brought in the East Texas oil field on October 6, 1930. This was considered the greatest oil field in the world and made Joiner the "father" of the East Texas oil field, hence the nickname "Dad."

WHIP-HANDLE DISPATCH

The "whip-handle dispatch" refers to a group of letters sent from Matamoros, Mexico, to Texas in 1836. The letters, which were hidden in a hollow whip handle, were written to warn the Texans that a large number of Mexican troops might invade Texas in the summer of 1836. The dispatch resulted in the issuance of a circular calling for the enlistment of the militia on June 20, 1836.

The Town without a Toothache

One small town that fits the profile of having an unusual claim to fame is the Panhandle town of Hereford, county seat of Deaf Smith County. This town was named for the massive herds of Hereford cattle in the region, which were significant enough to bring recognition to the town; however, its name gave way to a hidden asset that more nearly suited a publicist's formula for generating fame. It was discovered in 1941 that the children of Hereford had fewer cavities and other tooth defects than was known in other Texas regions. This was enough to establish bragging rights in any town. A study revealed that the town's water and soil had an exceptional amount of minerals, including natural fluoride.

This deterrent to tooth decay was a publicist's dream. The town became known as "the town without a toothache." The phenomenon, bolstered by the catchy boast, brought Hereford to the attention of the United States, as well as to the eyes of the world, through the many newspapers and magazines that picked up on the story.

MOBEETIE

Mobeetie, in Tyler County, was originally named Sweetwater. When the townspeople applied for a post office in 1879, they had to select a new name because there was already another Sweetwater. A tongue-in-cheek story goes that a local Indian offered his name, Mobeetie, which was later discovered to mean "buffalo chip." However, *The New Handbook of Texas* tells us that *mobeetie* is the Indian word for "sweet water."

ALIBATES

The Alibates Flint Quarries in the Texas Panhandle, near the Canadian River, became recognized as a national monument in 1965. The name Alibates came from the unintentional corruption of the name of a young cowboy who lived in a line camp at the quarry site in the late 1800s, Allie Bates.

RAGTOWN

When the Fort Worth and Denver Railroad was constructed across the Panhandle county of Potter in 1887, a construction crew camped on the property of Jess Jenkins, where a collection of buffalo hide huts and tents called "Ragtown" became the nucleus of present-day Amarillo. Henry B. Sanborn laid out a town site one mile southeast of Ragtown near Amarillo Lake, so named by Mexican herders because of the yellow color of the banks of the lake. The county seat remained Ragtown until 1893.

RANSOM CANYON (OR CAÑÓN DE LA RESCATE)

Southeast of the city of Lubbock, Texas, on the Brazos River in the vicinity of Yellow House Canyon, one can find one of the most unique links to the Native Americans in Texas: Ransom Canyon. This canyon on the Texas South Plains came by its name quite honestly. The canyon was known by the 1820s as a place where the Indians and New Mexicans met to barter for cattle and horses and trade for any captives. Captives were literally ransomed. These

meetings took place from July to September each year, and the practice continued into the 1840s.

Odessa

The first immigrants to Ector County found wide, rolling plains covered with mesquite and underbrush. Because of their resemblance to the steppes of Russia, an official of the newly built Texas and Pacific Railroad named the first settlement Odessa.

Old Glory

Texans are not strangers to patriotism, and this is vividly pointed out in Stonewall County where the town of Old Glory is located. The original name of the town was New Brandenburg, but anti-German sentiment during World War I was so strong that the citizens changed the name of their town to something they deemed more patriotic, hence, Old Glory.

Sweetwater

Sweetwater, another misnamed town, was founded on Sweetwater Creek in north-central Nolan County. Residents and anyone else familiar with the area know that the water there is anything but sweet!

Mineral Wells

One Texas town got its name from its main natural resource. For many years, hundreds of thousands of Texans and residents of nearby states came to Mineral Wells to drink and bathe in its water from natural wells, touted as an elixir that cured everything from paralysis to baldness. The town's bath houses were crowded with people suffering all types of disorders. The magical healing water was later dehydrated and the crystals packaged and sold as a patent medicine in drug stores throughout the country.

Named by Presidential Order

Burkburnett, fourteen miles north of Wichita Falls in Wichita County, was originally called Nesterville, as it was established by nesters on land that was part of Samuel Burk Burnett's vast Four Sixes ranch. It was later changed to Gilbert. In 1905 President Theodore Roosevelt was Burk Burnett's guest for a wolf hunt at the ranch. He had such a grand time he ordered the US Postal Service to change the name of Gilbert to Burkburnett in honor of his host. The town became the only community in Texas named by order of a president.

The Mysterious Rock Wall in Rockwall County

Rockwall County and its county seat, the town of Rockwall, were named after a rectangular outcropping of a subterranean dike or rock wall that can be seen in several places in the county. The wall, which encompasses an area of approximately twenty square miles, was discovered in 1852 by Terry Wade as he was digging a well. An article in a 1987 edition of the *Dallas Morning News* says that the wall extends five to forty feet below the ground. Much scientific study of the wall has been made, and the findings vary between it being a natural geological formation and the construction of a very early tribe. As part of a History Channel documentary in 2013, forensic geologist Scott Wolter concluded that the formation was created by layers of sand that settled and fractured in a unique pattern that looks strikingly similar to a man-made wall. To further complicate the mystery, geologist James Shelton noted several elements of the wall that appear to be "various linteled portals and archways complete with arch guiding springer stones." Given the property owner's reticence to allow large-scale excavation, this enigma may never be solved.

RESURRECTED NAMESAKE

Gleaning out Texas locations with unusual claims to fame requires a heap of looking, but in Texas, where excess seems to be the norm, we found one Texas city with not one but two (count 'em) genuinely unusual claims to fame. Wichita Falls, we are told by learned historians, "was named for a five-foot waterfall on the Wichita River," which died of natural causes more than a hundred years ago, some say. Texans disdain giving up such icons as a namesake, and civic pride demanded rehabilitation of the falls. In the middle 1980s city fathers decided that just as there was a rock wall in Rockwall, there should be a falls in Wichita Falls.

The original little falls was replaced by a more impressive, if man-made, falls in a park off US 287 near downtown, which was dedicated in 1987. Although in a different location than the original namesake, once again the city has a falls to match its name!

SKILLMAN STREET

The name of one of Dallas's busiest streets was changed due to a controversy. Prior to 1939, Skillman Street was named Charles Lindbergh Street. After moving to Europe in 1935, Lindbergh became acquainted with German field marshal Hermann Goering, head of Nazi Germany's air force. Lindbergh was invited to inspect the air force and afterward proclaimed it the finest air force in Europe. He was given a decoration by Adolf Hitler. After he returned to America, he became active in anti-war groups. According to a newspaper article at the time, Lindbergh was called by some "a Nazi agent in the U.S." Public opinion mounted against the American hero, and a movement was started that resulted in the Dallas City Council changing the name of the street to Skillman Street.

Swiss Avenue

The Works Progress Administration's guide to Dallas points out that what became one of Dallas's most fashionable addresses, Swiss Avenue, was so named because it was originally settled by a group of Swiss immigrants who came to Dallas after Swiss-born Dallas mayor Benjamin Long, a former La Reunion colonist, returned to Zurich in 1870 and persuaded a group of his countrymen to immigrate. Almost three dozen arrived in December of 1870 and built homes along what would become Swiss Avenue.

High Five

Today's "high-five" is a congratulatory gesture, particularly among athletes. But there was a time in Dallas when the term had more perilous implications. When the old city hall was located on the corner of Harwood and Main Streets, the Dallas city jail was located on the fifth floor. The jail was irreverently called "High Five," especially among those who were periodically incarcerated. At that time a threatening word of caution was, "If you don't stop this or that, you'll end up on High Five!"

"Panther City"

Although there are several versions given by historians as to how Fort Worth got the nickname "Panther City," the most accepted one is that in 1875 a Dallas newspaper reported, "Fort Worth is such a sleepy town that a panther was spotted dozing unmolested on Main Street!"

Where the West Begins

The city of Fort Worth's slogan, "Where the West begins," has no basis in any modern map markings. Those Texas cities located east of Fort Worth have come to think of that city as the demarcation line indicating the beginning of West Texas. The much-publicized slogan originated as the result of an Indian treaty. On September 29, 1843, General Edward H. Tarrant, for whom Tarrant County is named, and General George W. Terrell met with leaders of nine Indian tribes and signed the Bird's Fort Treaty, calling for Indians to end conflicts and establishing a line separating Indian lands from territory open for colonization. The Indians were not to enter lands west of that line, which was drawn through what is today Fort Worth. From this, Fort Worth adopted the slogan "Where the West begins." The city's cattle and cowboy culture lends credence to this descriptive slogan.

FORT SPUNKY

Fort Spunky, Texas, in southeastern Hood County, was originally Barnardville, named after Barnard's Trading House in 1847. It earned its current name after several fights broke out while the town was in the process of getting its post office.

ARP

A town in East Texas changed its name to benefit strawberry shippers. Arp, located in Smith County, was originally Strawberry, Texas. According to the *Handbook of Texas*, the name was changed to honor William Arp, a popular newspaper editor, and to aid strawberry shippers who had to label crates by hand. No doubt the shorter name reduced hand-lettering and thus increased the number of crates a shipper could label in a day.

SAXET

The backward (spelled) town of Saxet, Texas, was a farming and cattle-raising community in Shelby County and a shipping point on the Santa Fe Railroad. When the rail spur was removed, Saxet became a ghost town.

LITTLE ANGEL

The only county in Texas named for a woman is Angelina County. When Spanish friars established their mission, San Francisco de la Tejas, they took in an Indian child whom they named Angelina, which means "little angel." She was baptized and learned to speak Spanish; she later became an interpreter for Spanish explorers. The "little angel" also lends her name to a river and a national forest in Texas.

BATTLE NAMED FOR A SAINT

One famous Texas battle and river may owe their names to a European saint. The Battle of San Jacinto in which Texas won its independence took place along the banks of the San Jacinto River. The river was discovered on St. Hyacinth's Day, August 17. St. Hyacinth was known as the Apostle of Poland and died in 1257.

BON AMI

Bon Ami, in Jasper County, may very well be a clean place to live, but it was not named for the well-known scouring powder. Its name honors a Louisiana town by the same name. Clean or not, the town should be friendly: Its name, in French, means "good friend."

BEAUMONT

Among those Texas cities having an unsuitable name is Beaumont, founded in 1835 when its first reputed Anglo settler, Noah Tevis, sold fifty acres of land to the Thomas Huling Company through its agent, Henry Millard. A town site was laid out and named Beaumont, which means in French "beautiful mountain." Some say Millard named the city for a relative, while others say it was named for a slight elevation southeast of the city. The latter seems preposterous, since the highest elevation in Beaumont, located on the Gulf Coast, is thirty-six feet above sea level.

GRAYBURG

The Big Thicket town of Grayburg was established in 1805 by the Thompson-Ford Lumber Company, which built a lumber mill there. All the buildings were painted gray. Dr. F. L. Thompson, the company physician, suggested the town's name.

BRAZOS RIVER

One of the most interesting bits of geographic trivia involves the naming of the Brazos River. A very poignant legend, accepted by most historians as fact, involves the explorer Francisco de Coronado, who in 1716 with his expedition party wandered through Texas for days without water and would have died had a band of Indians not led them to a stream. Upon finding the water, a padre accompanying the expedition exclaimed, "Los brazos de dios!" which means "the arms of God!" Thus the life-saving body of water became the Brazos.

Y'ALL COME BACK NOW, YA HEAR?

The picturesque Hill Country town of Fredericksburg has a built-in friendly greeting for visitors. The first letters of the street names going east from the Vereins Kirche (church) spell "ALL WELCOME." Those going west spell "COME BACK." Locals explain that in the town's early days a lot of people came through Fredericksburg from the east on their way west, so they got their welcome from the east and an invitation to return as they departed westward.

SUNDAY HOUSES

The building of Sunday houses is believed to have originated in the Hill Country town of Fredericksburg. Upon their arrival, German settlers were given a half-acre town lot and a ten-acre farm plot. As there were no rural stores or churches, it was sometimes necessary for families to stay in town for several days at a time to trade and to attend church. This was especially true on special days such as Easter and Christmas. Some colonists used their town lots to build houses for staying over in town. These were called "Sunday Houses."

Pedernales River

One of Texas's most publicized rivers was named for the raw material used by the Indians in the making of weapons and tools. President Lyndon Johnson's beloved Pedernales River was so named because of the large amount of flint rock found there. The Spanish word for "flint," or "arrowhead," is *pedernal.*

Buda

The town of Buda (pronounced Byooda) was named for a widow who ran a hotel there. The word is a corruption of the Spanish word *viuda,* which means "widow."

Waterloo, Capital of Texas

For nearly two hundred years the name Waterloo has been synonymous with defeat and doom. Even *Webster's New World Dictionary* defines Waterloo as a "town in Belgium, scene of Napoleon's final defeat (1815); any disastrous or decisive defeat." Was it just a matter of geography or a cynical, political predestination that Austin, the Texas state capital, was originally named Waterloo? According to the *Texas Almanac,*

> *In 1839 the Texas Congress authorized a commission to select a permanent capital. It was to be north of the Old San Antonio Road between the Trinity and Colorado Rivers. It was to lie on major north-south, east-west trade routes and near the center of the state. The commission selected a site near Waterloo, an outpost on the Colorado River, about eighty miles north of San Antonio. The location was enhanced by its mild climate*

and plentiful water from nearby springs. In building the city, the town lots were sold in 1839 at a total income of $182,585, which practically paid for the government buildings under construction.

BEVO

One piece of Texas football lore involves the naming of the University of Texas team mascot, Bevo, a longhorn steer. The Longhorns have one of their fiercest rivals, the Texas A&M Aggies, to thank for it. Determined not to let UT forget a trouncing of 13–0, a group of Aggies kidnapped the steer and branded him with the score. The embarrassed Longhorns, unable to remove the brand, had a running-iron (used by rustlers to alter existing brands on livestock) made. By connecting the 1 and 3 to form a B, altering the dash to make an E, and inserting a V before the 0, the shameful score of 13-0 became the word "BEVO." Justifying that this could be a shortened form of "beeves," which means beef cattle, the Longhorns proudly adopted Bevo as the official name of their mascot.

DUBLIN

One might assume that the town of Dublin in Erath County was named after the famous city in Ireland. Though logical, that would be a wrong assumption. Dublin, founded in 1854 and named in 1860, was originally "Doublin," derived from the cry "double in," a warning that an Indian raid was imminent.

BIG LAKE

Big Lake, located in southern Reagan County, according to historians, has no big lake. It is named so because of a large depression two miles south of town that briefly becomes a lake in wet seasons, remaining filled for two or three days and then suddenly draining. The phenomenon is unexplained except for the theory that the water drains into an underground river.

Babyhead Mountain

Some Texas town names reflect the state's violent history. Such is the case with Babyhead Mountain in Llano County. This mountain was so named in 1850 when settlers discovered that raiding Comanche Indians had captured a white baby and put its head on a pole on the mountain.

Lost Maples State Park

Nestled in the Hill Country county of Bandera is a beautiful oddity. Lost Maples State Park is home to bigtooth maple trees that are "lost" because they are hundreds of miles south of usual maple habitat. Left over from an earlier, colder climate, the stand of maples still clings hard-headedly to the hills of southwest Texas, amid other vegetation long since changed to suit the warmer climate created when the last ice age ended.

Nueces River

The naming of one Texas river was influenced by the pecan. According to Texas history, the Spaniards discovered and named the Rio Nueces, which in Spanish means "river of nuts."

Weslaco

Cities in Texas are named in a variety of ways, some quite interesting. For instance, the town of Weslaco in the Rio Grande Valley was named for the W. E. Stewart Land Company (WESLaCo), which promoted the land development when the Missouri-Pacific Railroad came through Hidalgo County.

Mercedes

What's in a name? Sometimes a lot more than we think. Although the records reflect the Rio Grande Valley town of Mercedes was named for Mercedes Diaz, wife of Mexican president Porfirio Diaz, there may be more to the name than even the town's residents know. The original name of the community was Lonsboro, after Lon C. Hill, an agent and promoter. In 1905 the American Land and Irrigation Company changed the name, which may be more appropriate for other reasons. It is said that in the 1750s, the Spanish Crown gave generous land grants called "merceds" (meaning king's mercy) along the Rio Grande to Spaniards of "reliability," meaning wealthy ranchers. Mercedes was settled by Mexican ranchers in the late 1770s on early land grants.

Langtry

Though it is commonly believed that the town of Langtry, Texas, was named for the English actress Lillie Langtry, this is a piece of romantic lore that can be put to rest. Langtry, in Val Verde County, was established in 1881 when the Texas and New Orleans Railroad survey was made. The town was named for a civil engineer in charge of a group of Chinese railroad construction workers. However, Lillie Langtry allegedly did pay a visit to the town supposedly named for her by the eccentric Judge Roy Bean, but she arrived too late to meet the lawman who purportedly named his saloon, the Jersey Lily, in her honor. The judge had died ten months earlier, in March 1893.

Iraan

Iraan, though an oil town, has no connection with the Middle East country similarly named. Located five miles west of the Pecos River in Pecos County, Iraan became a town in 1928 when oil was discovered on a large ranch owned by Ira G. Yates. The name was chosen in a contest, the prize for which was a choice town lot. Iraan is a combination of the names Ira and Ann Yates.

Caballo Muerto Mountains

Although many people visit Big Bend National Park each year, few are aware that the mountains that form its eastern boundary are known locally as the "dead horse" mountains. Generally called the Sierra del Carmens, they are known in Brewster County as Caballo Muerto, "dead horse" in Spanish. The name came from an 1879 incident involving a surveying party from Presidio led by Captain Charles Nevill of the Texas Rangers. Under attack by Indians, the party killed their own horses rather than let them fall into the hands of the Indians.

El Paso

According to the *Handbook of Texas*, the original name of El Paso was Coon's Rancho, or Franklin, as it was sometimes called. Franklin Coons (or Coontz) was a Santa Fe trader who established a store on the Rio Grande in the area of present-day El Paso sometime prior to 1848. Three companies of US troops under Benjamin Beale were stationed at the Rancho in 1849. Coons became postmaster in 1850, and the settlement was officially named Franklin. With the incorporation of Moffinsville, Hart's Mill, and Concordia, the conglomerate became El Paso.

EL PASO DEL NORTE

The lowest pass through the Rocky Mountains is in Texas. The pass, earlier known by its Spanish name, "El Paso del Norte," is guarded by the present city of El Paso.

RED LIGHT DISTRICT

Reference books and lore alike attribute the origin of the term "red light district" to Texas. It's said to have been coined by railroad men after their practice of hanging signal lanterns by the front doors of local brothels while visiting.

THE CHICKEN RANCH

La Grange, county seat of Fayette County, is, without a doubt, most famous for a historic bordello, known throughout Texas as "the Chicken Ranch." The roots of this rural palace of sin can be traced back to 1844. According to published news reports, it operated part of its 130-year tenure with the knowledge and perhaps protection of a local lawman. During the Great Depression, the madam, Miss Jessie, began accepting chickens in payment to take care of two problems: customers lacked cash and the "girls" were going hungry. It wasn't long before Miss Jessie had a poultry and egg side business and her business was stuck with its unforgettable moniker.

Known as a place of initiation into manhood of Texas A&M freshmen, the house of ill repute was operated from 1952 by a madam known to customers as "Miss Edna." Edna Milton came to the ranch from Oklahoma in 1952 at the age of twenty-three. The famous Texas brothel was closed in 1973 as the result of an exposé by well-known Houston TV newsman Marvin Zindler. The attack on the bordello that had become a Texas institution generated so much publicity that it became the inspiration for a movie and a Broadway play, *The Best Little Whorehouse in Texas.*

NAMESAKES REMEMBERED

There are at least three of Texas's 254 counties that have county seats that, when combined with the county name, give the name of the person for whom the county was named. They are Gail, county seat of Borden; Anson, county seat of Jones County; and McKinney, county seat of Collin County. Gail Borden was an early publisher and inventor. Anson Jones was the last president of the Republic of Texas. Collin McKinney was an early settler.

UNCLE OSCAR

It sounds like a tall tale to say that the Academy Awards statuette, the Oscar, was named for a Texan, but although he was known to a limited few, Oscar's namesake was—according to the *Oxford English Dictionary*—indeed a Texan. Oscar Pierce had a niece who worked for the Academy of Motion Picture Arts and Sciences in Hollywood. When she saw the gold statue for the first time, she said, according to legend, "Why, it looks like my Uncle Oscar!"

ENTERPRISING TEXANS

THE LIFEBLOOD OF AMERICAN ECONOMICS IS ENTREPRENEUR-
ship, and history has proven that Texas is no exception. These
salt-of-the-earth, pull-yourself-up-by-your-bootstraps men and
women were willing to do what it took to make their dreams possible. They came up with workable solutions to problems, found
ways to fulfill needs where ones existed, and made leaps of faith
to take on new opportunities and challenges. Because of them,
we have comfortable beds, fences that keep cattle from straying,
and factories that continue to employ locals and pump money
into the state's economy—not to mention some of the world's
best sausages, soft drinks, and ice cream right here in our own big
back yard!

SAMUEL WALKER, REVOLVER DESIGNER

In the early days of the settling of Texas, the hand weapon of
choice for the settler facing a myriad of threats on the new frontier was the famous knife that bore the name of Alamo hero James
Bowie. This was to change in 1831 when Samuel Colt invented
his Colt revolver. Patented in February 1836, the first revolver
manufactured was a .34 caliber with a four-and-a-half-inch
octagonal barrel.

Sometime after the Texas Revolution, the Texas Rangers
began using the revolvers. One of the Rangers was Maryland-born
Samuel H. Walker, who had distinguished himself as an Indian
fighter in Georgia and Florida. After coming to Texas, he joined

Captain John C. Hays's Ranger company. Walker was sent to New York to deal with Samuel Colt regarding the purchase of arms for the Republic of Texas.

When he found Colt, he suggested certain modifications to the then popular "Texas revolver." He was responsible for the modified pistol known thereafter as the Colt Walker revolver. This pistol became the weapon of choice for the men of the Texas frontier.

GEORGE ADDISON KELLY

It was in a casual conversation in a Dallas retirement center that Margaret Kelly proudly told about her grandfather, George Addison Kelly, and the Kelly Plow company, which made the "Blue Kelly" plow. The Kelly Plow Company was the only full-line plow company in the Southwest. It began in 1843 when John Stewart began making crude plows in a shop near Marshall, Texas. In 1848 he moved to Four-Mile-Branch, later known as Kellyville. George Addison Kelly joined the company in 1852. By 1854 new foundry methods were introduced, and soon the plant was not able to supply the demand for plows. The firm became Kelly and Stewart in 1858 and added other products to its line. That same year, Kelly developed the Blue Kelly plow. It was so widely used in Texas that "Kelly" and "Blue Kelly" became household words synonymous with plow. Although the prophet Isaiah prophesied that the people would "beat their swords into plowshares and study war no more," just the opposite happened with the Kelly Plow Company. During the Civil War the company beat its plowshares into "swords," becoming part of the arsenal of the Confederacy and manufacturing cast-iron cannon balls. But after the war, suffering from the effects of the decline of the city of Jefferson and a plant fire in 1880, Kelly transferred the salvage to Longview in 1882. The third generation of the Kelly family managed the plant, which finally closed its doors in 1975. According to a historical marker erected at the site of the last plant, "Kelly Plow Works is reported to be the second oldest chartered industry in Texas."

Bone Piles

In the mid-1800s, one of the state's most lucrative, not to mention unusual, cash crops could be found literally at West Texas residents' feet. The availability of the item in demand kept a steady stream of wagons going to the plains and coming back loaded with, of all things, buffalo bones, which lay strewn across the desert, free for the picking. Fertilizer companies found that the sun-bleached bones could be used for a number of things and offered $8 to $10 a ton for them. Many tons of the bones were hauled from the principal supplying cities of Sweetwater, Abilene, Baird, Colorado, and Albany. Noted historian, author, and columnist A. C. Greene, who grew up in West Texas, remembers old-timers talking about buffalo bones stacked in piles longer than a city block in Abilene.

Gail Borden Jr.

One Texan to whom the world owes a debt of gratitude for his invention is Gail Borden Jr. Borden, a Galveston surveyor and newspaper publisher, began inventing in the mid-1800s. In 1853 he sought a patent for processing condensed milk in a vacuum, but it was 1856 before he received British and American patents. When the Civil War brought intensified demand for such milk, his company experienced such an upsurge in sales that Borden's success was assured. Borden also invented a process for condensing various fruit juices. Borden died in 1874.

Sarah Cockrell

An enterprising woman played an important role in Dallas history. In 1859 businesswoman Sarah Cockrell chartered the Dallas Iron and Bridge Co., which in 1872 completed the first iron bridge across the Trinity River. It was a toll bridge until it was purchased by Dallas County in 1882, at which time it became a free bridge.

VERSATILE STETSON

The inventor of this ubiquitous hat may not have been a Texan, but he was definitely inspired by Texans. The Stetson hat, icon of Texas style, was actually the creation of Yankee ingenuity. John B. Stetson of Philadelphia, who went west to regain his health in the 1860s, fashioned himself a big hat that would protect him from rain, sun, and wind. After his return to Philadelphia, Stetson made a hat that he called "boss of the plains" and sent it to Western dealers. The Texas Rangers adopted the hat and found it could be used for many things: to drink from, water one's horse, fan a campfire, blindfold a stubborn horse, smother a grass fire, and slap a steer. The hat also could serve as a target in gunfights. Then it could be brushed off for dress wear. Because of its versatility and durability, the hat became a distinguishing characteristic of the cowboy, as well as one of the popular features of Western fiction.

THE CHUCK WAGON

Taking things for granted provides little incentive for research. It is only when someone drops a contradictory bomb in your preconceived lap that you hustle off to the reference material in an effort to set the record straight about a particular matter.

Such was the case when I was alerted to the fact that my concept as to how the chuck wagon got its name might be wrong. I had always assumed that since "chuck" has been used for years as a synonym for food or grub, the name chuck wagon was a logical name for the vehicle used to transport food on a trail drive. Then came that contradictory "bomb" that set me to hitting the books!

One year, at the National Cowboy Symposium in Lubbock, a visitor announced to me that her grandfather had cowboyed on the famous Charles Goodnight ranch. She pointed out that rancher Goodnight had invented the prototype of the chuck wagon, which cowboys and other ranchers referred to as "Chuck's (for Charles) wagon" and later simply as the chuck wagon. The informative lady told us that Goodnight was fed up with delays caused by the cook having to juggle cooking utensils and food supplies each time a meal was served, as well as having to break down the small two-wheeled wagons sometimes used to transport food and utensils. So he loaded an ordinary chest of drawers into a wagon and took it to a wagon maker in a nearby town to see if it could be securely installed in the wagon so that utensils and foodstuffs could be easily managed. He also had a lid installed, which dropped down on a swinging leg to be used as a worktable for the cook.

Indeed, in the biography of Charles Goodnight, entitled *Charles Goodnight: Cowman and Plainsman,* by J. Evetts Haley, the researcher wrote,

> *He bought the gear of a government wagon, pulled it over to a woodworker in Parker County and had it entirely rebuilt with the toughest wood available, seasoned bois d'arc. Its axles were of iron instead of the usual wood, and in place of a tar bucket, he put in a can of tallow to be used in greasing. For the back end of the wagon he built the first chuck box he had ever seen, and recalled that it had been changed very little to this day. Its hinged lid let down on a swinging leg for a cook's table.*

Jon E. Lewis wrote in *The Mammoth Book of the West*: "Invented by Charles Goodnight, the chuck wagon was an adapted Conestoga, made of Osage orange [bois d'arc], the toughest wood Goodnight knew of, the wood Indians used for their bows [hence the French name bois d'arc or wood of the bow]."

In the book *The Cowboys,* William H. Forbis wrote, in speaking of the chuck wagon,

> *Credit for the ultimate design of the wagon belongs to cattle baron Charles Goodnight, who in 1866 rebuilt for his trail crew a surplus Army wagon, picked primarily for its extra-*

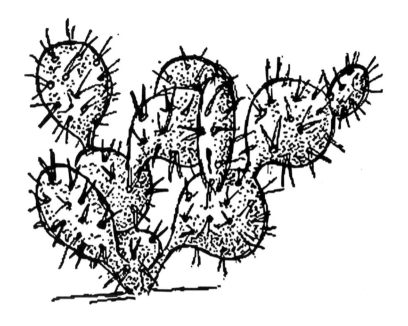

*durable iron axles. To the basic wagon bed, where bulk goods
such as foodstuffs and bedrolls were to be stored, Goodnight
added the already customary trail-drive appendages. But the
innovation that made the Goodnight wagon unique at the
time, and a useful prototype for all self-respecting wagons
that followed, was the design and installation of a chuck box.
Perched at the rear of the wagon, facing aft, it had a hinged lid
that let down on a swinging leg to form a worktable.*

JOHN WARNE "BET-A-MILLION" GATES

John Warne "Bet-a-Million" Gates was a barbed wire tycoon from
Texas who risked his fortune in the 1870s betting that barbed
wire would change the course of the frontier. Gates gave a demonstration in front of the Hord Hotel on the southwest corner of the
main plaza in San Antonio to show the effectiveness of barbed
wire. He made a corral with the wire and filled it with longhorn
cattle. The barbed wire successfully contained the livestock and

resulted in more orders for the wire than the factory could fill. The wire did, indeed, prove to make a difference in the old frontier and made Gates a rich man; after he was refused partnership in the company, he went into business for himself.

NOT-SO-FAMOUS INVENTOR

Many have cursed the Texas "black gumbo" soil for its bogging effect while trying to work it into some form of civilized use. But according to historians, the sticky black dirt had its virtues, among those the invention of the disc harrow and disc plow, two of agriculture's most valuable farm implements.

Norwegian immigrant Ole Ringness, who lived in Bosque County, encountered the miring mud and in the process of pushing his wagon out of the muck noticed the cupping action of the wheels. This gave him the idea for what became the disc plow and disc harrow. He developed working models of the implements and went to Washington, D.C., to see the patent office about the inventions.

While on a trip in 1872, Ringness died mysteriously; it is believed that his death was due to the fact he was carrying a large sum of money. Other references say that Ringness died from an illness. His family failed to pay the fee for his patent, and another plow company manufactured the disc plow and disc harrow, robbing the Norwegian inventor of the fame and fortune associated with his contribution to agriculture.

FRED HARVEY

After the transcontinental railroad was completed in the 1880s, passenger travel from Texas to California via the Southwestern states was a long, dusty, uncomfortable trip, with few opportunities for eating or getting a break from the tiring, upright seats. That was alleviated when Fred Harvey made a contract with Santa Fe Railroad officials to build restaurants and hotels at various stops along the way in Texas and throughout the Southwest. This made train travel more marketable, and Harvey Houses, as they were called, became a household word among train travelers.

DANIEL HAYNES

Folks around the world have a Texan, Daniel Haynes, to thank for a good night's sleep. In the 1880s, the Austin County settler invented the process and the machinery for manufacturing the cotton mattress. This was the forerunner of today's modern bedding. Haynes named his company for the town where he developed the machinery: Sealy, Texas. Thus began the Sealy Mattress Company.

THE FIRST HAMBURGER

America's most purchased and favorite food, the hamburger, was invented by a Texan. The hamburger got its start in the Henderson County town of Athens in the 1880s. Fletcher Davis served up a meat patty topped with mustard, a pickle, and onions, between two slices of bread. The sandwich caught on, and Davis introduced the hamburger at the World's Fair in St. Louis in 1904.

NOT A REAL DOCTOR

The reason there is no period after the Dr in Dr Pepper is, according to a company official, that it was dropped in the 1930s because the period designates the name as that of a medical doctor, which, of course, the soft drink is not! The oldest Dr Pepper bottling plant in the world is in Dublin in Erath County. Bill Kloster's nearly 130-year-old plant was opened in 1891 by Sam Houston Prim. The Prim family ran the plant for one hundred years before Bill Kloster inherited it in 1991. The drink was invented in Waco in 1885.

RED HOT CLAIM TO FAME LINKED TO EAST TEXAS TOWN

In 1897 Charlie Hasselback of German descent brought the hot links recipe to Camp County. Today they're known as Pittsburg

Hot Links. The sausage maker was first located in the old Maddox Building, where he sold the links over the counter for preparation at home. Information provided by the Pittsburg Chamber of Commerce advises:

> *Mr. Hasselback built an addition to the building in 1918 and started serving cooked links over the counter. With wooden counters and benches, the store was less than elaborate. Adding to the simplicity of the hot link business, the links were served with crackers on heavy market paper, and special sauce was provided in soda water bottles. The spicy fare was washed down with cold drinks offered in an assortment of flavors. The links were two for five cents, five for ten cents, and a dozen for a quarter. You could eat them there or carry them out, a custom that became popular with the housewife.*

Word about the links spread fast. Pittsburg had two railroad lines, and before long train crews were scheduling their stopovers in Pittsburg, where they could walk up the alley behind the building to eat their noon and evening meals. Truckers and traveling salesmen, hearing of the spicy links, started coming. Folks in nearby towns tried unsuccessfully to match the flavor of the linked sausage in their stores and markets.

So the name Pittsburg Hot Links was originated and continues in use to this day. Although the company has changed hands over the years, the same mouth-watering recipe drives the thriving business. You can now order the company's products online, but many argue that the Pittsburg restaurant is still the best place to stop for this town's iconic fare.

Texan Saved French Grape Industry

Thomas V. Munson of Denison is considered the father of the grape industry in Texas. In the 1890s Munson developed many new varieties of grapes and was responsible for many grapevine cuttings being shipped to France, where they were credited with saving the French vineyards from destruction by the aphid grape phylloxera.

WILLIAM GEBHARDT

Those who enjoy spicy food can thank Texas for much of their eating pleasure, as the first commercially packaged chili powder came from Texas. William Gebhardt, a German-born New Braunfels restaurateur, sold the first commercial chili powder in 1894. Before that, chili, which is the state dish, was served only when fresh chilies were available. By 1896 there was enough demand for the "eye-watering" spice that Gebhardt established a factory in San Antonio. Gebhardt added the nation's first canned chili con carne and canned tamales to his product line in 1911.

POST, TEXAS: TOWN MADE POSSIBLE BY BREAKFAST CEREAL

C. W. Post first came to Texas in 1895 and lived in Fort Worth. Post suffered from stomach and nervous disorders. In an attempt to get relief, he moved to Battle Creek, Michigan, where he entered the Battle Creek Sanitarium. His interest in health caused him to develop a cereal drink, which he named Postum, and found what now is the food giant General Food Corporation. He also developed breakfast cereals such as Post Toasties and Post Bran. Post was a millionaire many times over when he moved back to Texas in 1906. He purchased a quarter-million-acre ranch in Garza and Lynn Counties on the Texas high plains. At the center of this ranch, the businessman founded a town which he called Post City (now Post, Texas, county seat of Garza County).

Post divided the ranch into 160-acre fenced tracts of land with houses on them. Over a twelve-year period, C. W. Post colonized more than 1,200 families into the area. Post's health again failed in 1914, and on May 9, 1914, he committed suicide at his home in Santa Barbara, California.

Ringling Bros. Makes Fruitcake Popular

For more than 120 years, the Christmas holidays have been made tastier for families around the world thanks to a delicacy of Texas origin. Most Texans are familiar with "World Famous DeLuxe Fruitcake" from Corsicana's Collin Street Bakery. Most will be surprised to know that the success of this popular holiday cake can be attributed to the Ringling Brothers Circus!

The year 1896 was a decidedly special year for fruitcake connoisseurs. It was in that year that Texas immigrant Gus Weidmann, a master baker from Wiesbaden, Germany, teamed up with Tom McElwee in Corsicana, Texas, to establish the Collin Street Bakery and create the DeLuxe fruitcake now distributed worldwide. A company history reveals that while Gus worked his magic in the kitchen, Tom excelled at his forte, promoting the eye-appealing as well as palate-pleasing fruitcake.

By 1906 the demand of the bakery's clientele resulted in the bakery closing its original plant and opening a larger, more efficient facility. The new facility was of such an ambitious size that it allowed the partners to make the entire second floor into a hotel. Among those hosted by the bakery, to name but a few, were humorist Will Rogers, opera giant Enrico Caruso, professional boxer James "Gentleman Jim" Corbett, and a guest who turned out to be one of the bakery's major benefactors and whose name is synonymous with circus: John Ringling of Ringling Brothers Circus. It was this man's hotel visit that put Collin Street Bakery in the mail-order business, which is, next to its quality product, its real claim to fame. Old-timers at the bakery remember when Ringling's entire circus traipsed over to the bakery and ordered cakes for families and friends all over the world. This single event began an international Christmas event that continues today.

The bakery has expanded by adding four new locations and ships its famous fruitcake to 196 countries, as well as across the United States.

Hogs Credited with Oil Discovery

According to Big Thicket lore, J. F. Cotton's hogs should be given credit for rooting up more than just acorns. Saratoga, Texas, is credited with having the second oil strike in the Big Thicket. Following the big discovery of oil at Sour Lake, residents of the Big Thicket were conscious of this newly developing resource around them. When Fletcher Cotton noticed his hogs coming out of an area of the thicket slick with a glossy substance, he followed them and discovered the same tell-tale signs that had existed at Sour Lake before oil was discovered. Sour Lake had been a health spa known for its medicinal springs. Neighboring Saratoga Springs took its name from the famous New York spa. Sour Lake continued as a health resort until oil was discovered in 1901. The first producing well in Saratoga in 1903 was brought in two years after the famous gusher Spindletop. Mr. Cotton's hogs really "brought home the bacon."

The Ezekiel Airship

Although the East Texas town of Pittsburg is known far and wide throughout Texas by sausage aficionados for its extra spicy hot link sausage, it has another claim to fame that warranted the state of Texas to erect a historical marker in the town. It was in this town that Baptist preacher Burrell Cannon (no relation to the author) built the Ezekiel airship, billed by the Pittsburg Chamber of Commerce as "man's first powered flight." While this claim might be disputed by some, enough interest was generated in the airplane, actually more of a helicopter, to warrant the historical marker.

The airship was built by the Reverend Cannon in the Pittsburg Machine Shop one year prior to the Wright Brothers' historic flight in 1903 at Kitty Hawk. The odd-shaped craft, according to its publicists, "flew the skies over Pittsburg."

This may be somewhat of an exaggeration. The craft made its first flight in 1902 from a pasture that belonged to the owner of the machine shop where the craft was built. It could be said that the craft was divinely inspired. Reverend Cannon, a lifelong student of the Bible, was particularly intrigued by the Bible's account of Ezekiel's vision of God and strange flying creatures that were propelled by wheels (Ezekiel 1:16–19).

From such description an idea was born. Reverend Cannon's airship had large, fabric-covered wings. It was propelled by an engine that turned four sets of paddles mounted on wheels. Publicity says that those present at the first flight reported that when the engine first started, "the aircraft lurched forward for a short distance, rising vertically into the air. It traveled a few feet and then began to drift for a short distance." The description goes on to say, "The airship was vibrating considerably, so the engine was turned off and it came back to earth." The first flight was hardly flying through the skies over Pittsburg, as was reported.

The airship was being shipped by rail to St. Louis where it was to be exhibited at the World's Fair. A storm, however, blew it off the flatbed car near Texarkana, Texas, and it was destroyed. Legend has it that Reverend Cannon said, "God never willed that the airship would fly; I want no more to do with it!" He left it where it lay.

Cannon had formed the Ezekiel Air Ship Manufacturing Company, and stock in the airship company sold around Pittsburg for $25 per share. A replica, built by the Pittsburg Optimist Club in the 1980s, can be seen at the North Texas Rural Heritage Center and Depot Museum in Pittsburg.

TEXACO

The company known for the old jingle "You can trust your car to the man who wears the star" had its beginning at Sour Lake, Texas, in south central Hardin County near the Big Thicket. The town was named for the mineral springs that fed the lake. It was first settled in 1835, but long before white settlers, Indians made use of its mineral springs and the pitch found around the oil seepage along the lake's shore. As early as 1850 it was a health resort with good accommodations for health seekers, including Sam Houston, and continued to be so until the discovery of oil in 1902. The Texas Company, Texaco, had produced about ninety million barrels of oil from its Sour Lake field by 1948.

LIFE HASN'T ALWAYS BEEN PEACHES AND CREAM IN BRENHAM

The Washington County seat of Brenham, known best as the home of the Blue Bell Creamery that produces the popular Blue Bell ice cream, hasn't always enjoyed the peaceful, pastoral image projected by the creamery today. Established in 1844 and incorporated in 1858, the peaceful town found itself embroiled in discord when, during the Reconstruction period following the Civil War, the town was made a military post. Federal soldiers and citizens became involved in a controversy that resulted in a partial burning of the town in 1867. Military rule lasted until 1869.

Many Germans settled in Brenham during the Reconstruction period. The Blue Bell Creamery, named for the flowers that blanketed the area, opened in 1907. Blue Bell still makes and delivers its much-sought-after products from Brenham and has expanded its manufacturing to plants in Alabama and Oklahoma.

EDDIE RICKENBACKER

Early automobile racer and war hero aviator Eddie Rickenbacker came to Dallas in 1908 or 1909 to represent Clinton D. Firestone, whom he had met as a successful car racer, in his automobile company, Firestone Columbus Buggy Company. Rickenbacker frequently demonstrated these early automobiles on Dallas's Chalk Hill to show the prospective buyer how the car could handle inclines. One anecdote told about the aviator says that while he was demonstrating an auto to a customer, the car couldn't pull the hill in first gear. Rickenbacker supposedly turned the negative into a positive by slamming on the brakes and telling the customer, "Just look at those brakes, how they hold on this hill." It is said that the customer bought the car the same day.

JOHN W. SHARY

John W. Shary was known as the father of the Texas citrus industry. He planted the first commercial citrus orchard in the Rio Grande Valley in 1911, and the town of Sharyland is named after him.

MADE IN TEXAS

Old-timers in Dallas might remember when the Ford Motor Company had a plant on East Grand Avenue and how each car that rolled off the assembly line proudly bore a decal in the rear window proclaiming "Built in Texas by Texans." This method of manufacturing bragging wasn't a new one, however. In the early 1900s, the Wichita Falls Motor Company, which manufactured trucks, carried the advertisement "Made in Texas for Texas Roads."

GUS BAUMGARTEN

Bakers across America owe a debt of gratitude to the German immigrant Gus Baumgarten of Schulenberg. Baumgarten invented the oven thermostat, which regulates heat for baking. He became involved in a project to utilize cottonseed meal for baking; however, when government agents came to see his progress, they became more intrigued with the thermostat he had developed. As a result, they prescribed that all ovens made in the United States were to include a thermostat to regulate heat.

HUMBLE BEGINNINGS
The Mobley Hotel in Cisco, Texas, was bought in 1919 by Conrad Hilton and became the first hotel in the Hilton chain.

FORT WORTH'S CASA MAÑANA, A PRODUCT OF NEIGHBORLY RIVALRY
In 1924 a permanent Texas Centennial committee was approved to make plans to celebrate the one hundredth anniversary of Texas independence. Dallas was chosen as the site for the Centennial celebration. The selection of Dallas inflamed the already existing friendly rivalry between that city and its westerly neighbor, Fort Worth. It especially ruffled the feathers of businessman and Fort Worth booster Amon Carter. That rivalry spawned a project that is alive and well today in the "city where the West begins." The rivalry helped bring about Casa Mañana (House of Tomorrow). The year-round, air-conditioned, aluminum-domed, theater-in-the-round was not the original Casa Mañana.

Already rankled by the selection of Dallas as the site for the Centennial celebration, Amon Carter signed the famous Broadway producer Billy Rose at $1,000 a day for one hundred days to produce the "show of shows" for Fort Worth.

History of the Casa tells us how in a few days a pasture was transformed into forty magic acres housing the largest revolving stage and café in the world. It accommodated four thousand diners and dancers. It ran for four consecutive years.

Today, only memories remain of its grandeur. In 1945 a bond election included $500,000 for building a recreation center and amphitheater; however, financial considerations caused the matter to be delayed for twelve years. The project was brought to life again in 1957 by the late James Snowden, Fort Worth oilman. He was instrumental in moving the city council to create a nonprofit corporation to build today's theater-in-the-round. Construction began in March of 1958; 114 days later the theater opened its first season. Casa Mañana is now home to one of the largest children's theater schools in the United States.

John Mitchell

One first that all Texans will appreciate, being keenly aware of the state's reputation for hot summers, is the development of the first automobile air-conditioning by Dallasite John Mitchell of the Frigicar Company. Mitchell in 1939 installed the first automobile air conditioner in the car of the president of Packard Motor Company.

Popeye's Favorite Place

During the 1950s Texas was the nation's leading spinach-producing state. Production was centered in the "winter garden" area of South Texas. At the time, 16,000 acres yielded 2,062,000 bushels valued at $3,608,000. A statue of the cartoon character Popeye was erected at Crystal City, the site of one of the world's largest spinach canneries.

"Uplift Town" Known for Brassiere Factory

McLean, located thirty-five miles from Oklahoma in Gray County, was the last Texas town bypassed by Interstate 40, resulting in its losing its spot on the fabled Route 66. But this is not the town's most unusual claim to fame. This town was once known as "the Uplift Town" because of a brassiere factory built in McLean in the late 1950s. Marie Foundations was important to the region's economy because of employment opportunities.

The factory building is now occupied by Delbert Drew's Devil's Rope and Route 66 Museum. The barbed wire exhibited is a far cry from the comfort of the ladies' undergarments once turned out there!

ON THE MAP

ALTHOUGH TODAY IT'S CLEAR WHERE TEXAS'S BORDERS ARE (even without a wall in sight), in its history these boundaries have been fluid—sometimes literally, depending on which river we're discussing. But who knew that the capital of Missouri used to be in Texas or that the Philippines once claimed this land as its own? You didn't, either? Read on . . .

NUEVES FILIPINAS

For a time, Texas and the Philippines bore the same name. Nueves Filipinas (New Philippines) was the name for Texas about 1716. Don Martín de Alarcón was appointed governor of the New Philippines. Henderson Yoakum's *History of Texas* shows a map of Spanish Texas with the New Philippines clearly marked.

MEXICO'S CHANCE TO RECLAIM TEXAS

Some eighty-one years after Texas won her independence from Mexico and seventy-two years after Texas became a state, Mexico was given a chance to reclaim it through a bizarre plot hatched in Germany. According to the *World War One Source Book,* Germany's secretary of state, A. Zimmerman, sent a coded cable to Germany's ambassador to Mexico, Von Eckhardt, on January 19, 1917, which contained an unusual proposal: In the event of hostilities between Germany and the United States, Germany should assist Mexico in recapturing their lost territories of Texas, New Mexico, and Arizona, and Japan should be invited into the Mexican-German alliance. British Naval Intelligence intercepted and decoded the cable and passed it to Walter Page, US ambassador to Britain, and Page forwarded it to the US State Department. President Wilson published the note on March 1, 1917. This caused widespread indignation in the United States, and although Mexico and Japan denied it, this event, along with other German intrigue, had a considerable effect on political and public opinion and paved the way for a US declaration of war on Germany on April 16, 1917.

RICE HOTEL

For many years, thousands of visitors to Houston have lodged themselves at the Rice Hotel without realizing it was built on the same site that once contained the capitol of the Republic of Texas. Before Houston was fully developed, the Allen Brothers offered, at their own expense, to build a building to be used by the government if their city was selected as the republic's capital. They proceeded to build a two-story building that served as capitol from 1837 to 1839.

REPUBLIC OF THE RIO GRANDE

Texas's victory of independence from Mexico may have influenced the formation of another republic. Not much is written about the Republic of the Rio Grande because it existed for less than a year, but an effort on the part of the federalist leaders in Tamaulipas, Nuevo Leon, and Coahuila to break away from the centralist government of Mexico in 1840 formed a new confederation that included part of Texas.

From 1835, when Antonio López de Santa Anna, then a centralist, became president of Mexico, leaders throughout the nation attempted to force a return to the federalistic constitution of 1824. The sentiment was particularly strong in the northern states of Mexico, and when they failed to succeed at their quest, the northern federalists set out to win independence from the Mexican Republic. Texas's recent success at winning de facto independence probably influenced their action. On January 17, 1840, they con-

vened at Laredo, Texas, and declared independence from Mexico and staked their territorial claim on the areas of Tamaulipas and Coahuila north to the Nueces and Medina Rivers, respectively. After several military confrontations, on November 6, 1840, the federalists capitulated, and the republic, which had lasted less than a year, came to an end.

COMMONSENSE SECESSION

While it is generally believed that Texas's secession from the Union in 1861 was the state's only experience with secession, the formation of Rockwall County proves this is not so. Settlement of Rockwall County began in 1846 when the area was part of Kaufman County. Because of inconvenience in reaching the county seat, settlers decided to secede from Kaufman County and organize their own county. It was, according to local historians, a bloodless secession. By setting up their own county, the settlers made it convenient to handle county business. The separate county was organized in 1873, and Rockwall was made county seat.

CENTER CITY

Although modern cartography differs to some degree, Center City in Mills County was so named because it is the geographical center of Texas.

Texas Ski Hill

Texas is thought of by many as flat and prairie-like (and some parts indeed are), but at one time Texas had some great slopes for downhill skiing. An 1836 map shows that the Republic of Texas included that portion of Colorado in which is located one of today's most popular ski resorts, Crested Butte.

Border Dispute

Before Texas won its independence from Mexico in 1836, the Nueces River was considered the border between the two lands. The Texans, dictating the peace terms to Mexican dictator General Santa Anna, put the border at the Rio Grande River. When he balked, they showed him a hangman's rope and he agreed. This was never accepted by the Mexican government, however, which led to the Mexican-American War of 1846. The border was not agreed upon until Mexico signed the treaty of Guadalupe Hidalgo in 1848.

Inland Port

One Texas town was a shipping port second only to Galveston, and it wasn't even located on the coast! The quaint and very picturesque town of Jefferson, on Caddo Lake in East Texas, was at one time known as the "Riverport to the Southwest." By using a chain of lakes and bayous to the Red River, flat-bottomed steamboats could travel up the river to Jefferson and then to Shreveport, enabling the shipping and receipt of goods without overland transport.

Because of the ease of water transport, Jefferson's economy became particularly robust after the Civil War, when nearly seventy-five thousand bales of cotton passed through the port each year. However, subsequent events that resulted in a change of available waterways made the town inaccessible to shipping; furthermore, the newly constructed Texas and Pacific Railway bypassed Jefferson altogether.

One Big State

Texas's immense size is best illustrated by the fact that the Panhandle city of Dalhart is closer to the capitals of four other states (New Mexico, Oklahoma, Kansas, and Colorado) than it is to the Texas capital in Austin. Mileages are as follows: Dalhart to Austin, 537; Dalhart to Santa Fe, New Mexico, 327; Dalhart to Oklahoma City, 309; Dalhart to Denver, Colorado, 471; Dalhart to Topeka, Kansas, 489.

Two Cities in Three States

Texas has two cities that, combined, are located in *three* states. Texhoma, in northeastern Sherman County on the Texas-Oklahoma border, was established in 1900 and is Texas's northernmost city. Its banks, post office, and much of its business district are on the Oklahoma side. Texarkana, in Bowie County, straddles the Texas-Arkansas state line. While commercially one city, Texarkana has two sets of councilmen and city officials. There is a cooperative arrangement for joint operation of the fire department and other services. The federal building has the distinction of being the only building of its kind situated in two states, and the post office is the only one in the nation serving two states. The address: Texarkana USA 75502. A marker in front of the building is a favorite spot for pictures, as it enables one to be photographed in two states at once.

The County Lost to Oklahoma

On February 8, 1860, the Texas state legislature passed an act providing for the organizing of Greer County. However, with the onset of the Civil War, nothing was done to establish a county government. In July of 1886 the settlers of Greer County finally established a government with Mangum as the county seat. A jail, two post offices, and a school system were established.

Then a boundary dispute arose between Texas and the United States as to the ownership of the county. Errors in the maps used to set the boundary led to the dispute, as well as confusion over which fork of the Red River was the proper boundary line. In 1890 President William Henry Harrison approved an act authorizing the organization of Oklahoma as a territory, and a suit against the State of Texas was filed for a final settlement of the dispute of ownership of Greer County.

Although a strong argument was made by Texas, which had settled the area and administered it for thirty-five years, in 1896 the Supreme Court ruled that Greer County was a part of the United States. In 1906 Greer County became a part of the state of Oklahoma. This area Texas lost to Oklahoma, "X-Tex land," is all of Oklahoma southwest of the North Fork of the Red River.

Pueblos Cross the Border

The oldest settlements in Texas are the missions and pueblos of Ysleta and Socorro, located near present-day El Paso. They were established in 1862 in Mexico across the Rio Grande from El Paso and remained in Mexico until the flooding of the Rio Grande in the early nineteenth century moved them to the Texas side of the international boundary set by the treaty ending the Mexican-American War. The United States obtained these pueblos through a "land grab" assisted by Mother Nature.

Similarly, San Elizario, a town located about twenty miles south of El Paso on the Rio Grande River, was probably on the Mexican side of the Rio Grande but ended up on the American bank when the river's course changed. US troops were stationed there in 1850, and the California Column made its headquarters there in 1862. San Elizario was the county seat of El Paso County from 1850 until 1876, when it moved to Ysleta.

Rio Grande

The "daddy of all Texas rivers," the Rio Grande, has been known at different times and various places along its course as Rio del Norte, Rio San Buenoventura, Rio Turbio, and Rio Bravo. The name Rio Grande was given by explorer Juan de Onate, who arrived at its banks near today's El Paso in 1598. From source to mouth, the river drops twelve thousand feet to sea level. The length of the river depends on the method of measurement and varies yearly as its course changes; the latest International Boundary and Water Commission figure is 1,896 miles. Again depending on the method of measurement, the Rio Grande is the fourth- or fifth-longest river in North America and is Texas's longest river. It irrigates a broad valley of central New Mexico dating from the 1600s, the oldest irrigated area in the United States. Through the Big Bend the Rio Grande flows through three successive canyons: Santa Elena, Mariscal, and Boquillas. The river drains more than forty thousand square miles of Texas.

THE SABINE AS A BORDER

When Texans think of an international border, as related to Texas, they automatically think of the Rio Grande as the border between Mexico and Texas. One other Texas river has seen service as an international border. The Sabine, which means cypress in Spanish, makes up two-thirds of the border between Louisiana and Texas. The 360-mile-long river served as international border between the United States and Spain, the United States and Mexico, and the United States and the Republic of Texas.

THE REAL LONESOME DOVE

Lonesome Dove, Texas, or the Missouri Colony as it was called, is much more than just the namesake of Larry McMurtry's Pulitzer Prize–winning novel and the TV miniseries it spawned. The real Lonesome Dove, with its blacksmith shop, school, church, and restaurant with a "Woodmen of the World" hall upstairs, existed on the edge of the Cross Timbers. Many of the settlement's residents moved to nearby Grapevine when the railroad came through there. Today the community site near Dallas–Fort Worth International Airport is dotted with high-priced homes separated by an occasional old home and the bustling shopping centers serving the new inhabitants. The one remaining recognizable remnant of the much-publicized fictional town is the red brick Lonesome Dove Baptist Church and its adjoining cemetery, both carved out of a grove of age-old trees that were once part of the Cross Timbers. The church was established in 1846 by a group of settlers from Platte County, Missouri, who came to Texas by ox-drawn wagons and formed the Missouri Colony.

Although more than one version exists as to how the church, and thus the community, got its name, the one most accepted and most logical is that at the time of its establishment the Lonesome Dove Baptist Church was the first church in Tarrant County and the only Protestant church between the Trinity River and the Pacific coast. Metaphorically speaking, Christ (the dove) was understandably a lonesome figure. It was also said that the church's committee selecting a name heard the cooing of a mourning dove during their meeting. This, they reported, sounded very lonesome and they thought their selection of a name very fitting. Being so far out on the western frontier, the area at the time was not lacking a "shoot 'em up" atmosphere; church records reveal that the original wooden structure was burned by unfriendly Indians who were killed after being caught.

Another historical event in Lonesome Dove's past was when the church's first clerk was gored by a bull buffalo. He had the dubious honor of being Tarrant County's first surgery patient. The Lonesome Dove cemetery is the resting place of some of Tarrant County's first elected officials after the county's organization in 1850. Also reflecting the dangers of this time on the Texas prairie is the church's report that the walls at the back of the building were often lined with members' guns, brought to church in case of sudden Indian attack. Although author McMurtry's fictional Lonesome Dove was exciting, the facts chronicled by past inhabitants of the real community reflect the true pioneer spirit on the North Texas prairie more than 150 years ago.

TREATY OAK

Of all of Austin's landmarks, few have received as much publicity as the Treaty Oak. The famous tree is a five-hundred-year-old live oak with a branch spread of 110 feet. It stands on property on Baylor Street that was acquired by the City of Austin in 1937. The tree was a landmark and popular picnic spot for citizens of Austin before the city engulfed it in the 1880s. The name comes from a local story that Stephen F. Austin signed a treaty with the Indians under its branches, but there is little foundation for this belief.

In 1989 the tree received nationwide attention when someone tried to kill it by poisoning it. The person attempting to destroy the old landmark was convicted and given a nine-year jail sentence. Although it was necessary to prune about two-thirds of its branches to save it, the tree survived the attempt on its life. Its dead branches were pruned out and sliced into wafers to be sold with certificates of authenticity and the proceeds used to plant other oaks as a living memorial to the famous landmark.

THE MANY LIVES OF THE ALAMO

The Alamo has been used for a number of things throughout its long history. Its walls have housed troops, Indians, Tejanos, and squatters. It was San Antonio's first hospital, from 1806 to 1812. It has been used as a Masonic lodge, a jail, a commercial store, and a warehouse.

RIVER WALK SAVED FROM THE GUTTER

Before the San Antonio River was included in a federally funded beautification program that resulted in today's Paseo del Rio, or River Walk, some of the city's businessmen wanted to convert the downtown section of the river into a sewer and build a street on top of it.

TAYLOR COUNTY COURTHOUSE

Taylor County can boast of having a courthouse held together by cannonballs. The old Taylor County courthouse and jail was built in 1879 in Buffalo Gap, which was the county seat prior to 1880, when it was moved to Abilene. The building was built on unstable soil, so the builder hollowed out pockets in the limestone blocks and put in cannonballs hauled from Vicksburg, Mississippi, after the Civil War to lock the blocks together. It is said that after a hundred years, no cracks can be found in the old building, which is now part of the nonprofit educational site Buffalo Gap Historic Village.

VOTING UNDER THE INFLUENCE

One unverified but interesting morsel of Fort Worth trivia is the story of how the town became the Tarrant County seat. There are those who say that Fort Worth won the election to become the county seat over its nearby rival Birdville by dubious means. According to local lore, Fort Worth stole Birdville's whiskey stash, brought in bogus voters, and then freely dispensed the liquor to influence their votes in the November 1856 election.

BLACK SETTLEMENTS

Two of Dallas's early communities were black settlements whose names have been all but forgotten, although the areas are well known. Little Egypt, known also as Mission Hill, dates back to Civil War days. The center of this black community was Egypt Chapel Baptist Church, which was sold in 1962. Little Egypt was a thirty-five-acre tract located north of Northwest Highway bounded by Easton Road and Ferndale. Elm Thicket (or Ellum Thicket) was a community of freed slaves located between University Park on the east and Love Field on the west.

TRUMAN

Thousands of commuters stream past the corner of Interstate 30 (old Highway 80) and Gus Thomasson Road daily without being aware that this location was once the town of Truman, Texas, now a part of Mesquite. It is safe to say that only a handful of people in that city know about Truman, with the exception of the few former residents of Truman and a few public officials. The story of Truman is a simple one and typical of many small communities with a heart and a history that were gobbled up by larger cities with better capability to serve their residents. While the name may be lost, the story of the town of Truman is worth passing on to those with an interest in preserving our heritage.

According to newspaper clippings, on November 21, 1945, Mrs. E. H. Hopkins christened the town of Truman into existence with a milk bottle. She was quoted as saying that the reason she used a bottle of milk was "because so many of the community's residents were Baptists." The sign she christened read "Dallas city limits 7 miles." The dedication included the reading of numerous letters of congratulations, and Dallas postmaster J. Howard Payne read a telegram from President Harry Truman stating, "I am deeply conscious of the honor which the new community in Dallas County is according me in giving my name to the town of Truman. I send my hearty felicitations and warmest personal greetings to all of the townspeople—Harry S. Truman." The community had been called by at least five other names prior to being named Truman: Chitlin Switch, The Gravy, Deanville, North Mesquite, and Mesquite Tap. The trading post owned by E. C. Cogburn was the stop for a bus line that called the place Mesquite Tap before it became Truman. The community had a population of about two hundred with several businesses and a church. Mrs. Hopkins, the self-appointed historian of Truman, said in an interview that "there were only eight telephone lines in the area, and when your phone would ring the eight-phone party line would listen in."

The main reason the community incorporated in the first place was in an attempt to get water, telephone, and utility service. Truman had no post office, and requests for letters to receive a Truman postmark couldn't be met. The first mail in Truman was marked RFD (rural free delivery) and delivered by Jack McDonald, who was a champion cross-country bicycle rider. Although the town honoring the president received a lot of national attention, including a write-up in *Time* magazine, it was soon annexed into Mesquite. But according to the Mesquite Public Library, there are still a few homes that date from when the town was Truman.

TOWN, POPULATION: 5, FAMOUS FOR ITS SMOKESTACK

The former Erath town of Thurber, located between Mineral Wells and the city of Ranger, has the rare distinction of being known for a red brick chimney. Thurber was established in 1886 as a coal-mining town. When the mine became so unproductive that the coal company couldn't meet its payroll, it was sold to the Texas and Pacific Coal Company and the town was named Thurber.

After the discovery of oil in nearby Ranger, workers in Thurber went on strike for higher wages, influenced by wages paid to oil workers in Ranger. By this time the town, including homes, churches, and schools, had been built for its workers by the coal company and was called Texas and Pacific Coal. The company converted to brick making and moved to Fort Worth.

With no industry the town closed in 1933 and became virtually a ghost town. The last remaining evidence that the town was once a thriving industrial town is a red brick smokestack erected in 1909 as part of the coal company's power plant. A restaurant was built near the relic of a bygone era. A marker at the 128-foot-tall smokestack tells the story of "the most important mine-site in Texas for 30 years." The population sign, which once boasted ten thousand, now reads five.

The family that owns the Smokestack Restaurant—Randy Bennett; his wife, Andrea; and their three offspring, Robbie, Rusty, and Mollie—are not only its proprietors but constitute the town's total population. The old relic-turned-restaurant can be seen for several miles from several highways.

TOWN'S CLAIM TO FAME YIELDS CLUE TO SHAMEFUL US INDIAN POLICY

If, in your travels through West Texas, you bypassed the business district of the Scurry County seat of Snyder, you missed seeing one of the state's most obviously unusual claims to fame. On the town square stands a statue of a buffalo. Not just any of the thousands of proud animals that once called the South Plains home, this statue commemorates the shooting of one of a mere handful of white buffaloes known to have been seen in the American West! The animal was killed ten miles northwest of Snyder by one of America's most prolific buffalo hunters, J. Wright Mooar.

Mr. Mooar was born in 1851 in Vermont. As a youth, Mooar had heard about buffalo hunting in Kansas. By the time Mooar was nineteen, he had saved enough money to form a party of six men and go to Kansas to hunt buffalo. Buffalo meat was sold to the army to feed troops and to railroad construction crews, but the hides were considered worthless. Mooar shipped some hides to his brother, John, in New York City, and there they found a good market. John joined his brother in Kansas, and they worked together to hunt buffalo and market their hides. Mooar set up the first buffalo hunting camp in the Texas Panhandle in 1871. A story of the famed buffalo hunter says that his most serious problem was the lack of a gun suitable for buffalo hunting. He contacted the Sharps Rifle Company of Bridgeport, Connecticut, who designed and made a gun for $150. The gun became famous as "the Big 50." Later the Sharps .44 became a favorite with buffalo hunters.

On October 4, 1876, Mooar and a party of four men set up a hunting camp in Scurry County, about ten miles northwest of Snyder on Deep Creek. After surveying the country one day, Mooar returned to camp about sunset. The sun reflected off a white object in the midst of a buffalo herd. "I quickly saw it was a white buffalo," Mooar said. "Only seven white buffalo were ever seen or killed by white hunters, records show, and I had killed one of them in Kansas." Taking another hunter, Dan Dowd, Mooar slipped down Deep Creek toward the herd. Mooar dropped the white buffalo with one shot. He had the buffalo dressed and kept the hide, which was displayed at the St. Louis World's Fair in 1904. The hide was then displayed in Mooar's home. Experts claim that the odds in the 1800s of an albino calf being born were one in ten million. By 1877 buffalo hunting had died out, and Scurry County's first settler, J. Wright Mooar, turned to cattle raising.

It was while investigating this event that gives Snyder its unusual claim to fame that we discovered what could be considered by some "another shameful example of the US policy toward the American Indian." In a conversation with Mrs. Judy Hays, granddaughter of J. Wright Mooar, who owns the hide of Snyder's famous white buffalo, we learned some interesting and disturbing facts about her grandfather's hunting reputation. Mrs. Hays told us that while he did sell buffalo hides, he told her that he hunted buffalo as an agent of the US government. The American government paid to have the buffaloes slaughtered to get rid of the main food source of the Indians in hopes the Indian problem would dissipate. She said she did not know for whom or what agency her grandfather worked or how he was paid while purging the land of the buffalo. Research shows that Ulysses S. Grant was president while Mr. Mooar was making a name for himself as a buffalo hunter.

The Consequences of an Unpaid Debt

But for an unpaid medical bill, Tioga, Texas, might have become Autry Springs, Texas. Orvon Grover Autry (better known as Gene Autry) was born in Tioga—about an hour's drive north of Dallas—on September 27, 1907. In 1936 Autry made an offer to spend the necessary funds to rejuvenate his ailing birthplace. His desire was that the town, which had been noted for its mineral springs, would change its name to Autry Springs.

Tiogans shunned the singing cowboy's suggestion and his request to be immortalized on the Texas map. City fathers, at the urging of local physician E. Eugene Ledbetter, from whom, it is said, Autry got his first name, "Gene," rejected Autry's suggestion. According to legend, the doctor was bitter because the sharecropper Autry family hadn't paid the doctor's fee for the delivery of the future film and recording star, said to have been all of $25. The singing cowboy had to settle for his memory being preserved by the Oklahoma town of Berwyn, where he grew up as a youth. The town, in 1941, voted to change its name to Gene Autry, Oklahoma. His Tioga birthplace did eventually honor the star with a street bearing his name.

HELL HATH NO FURY LIKE A SPURNED STONEMASON

If you ever pass through Waxahachie, the beautiful Ellis County courthouse is well worth a sightseeing stop. But look closely, because this building, according to some, has a story to tell. Local legend tells us that Harry Herley, the stone carver who was employed to sculpt the columns of the 1896 courthouse and who boarded with the Frame family in that city, fell in love with the Frames' daughter, Mable. He used Mable Frame as a model for the faces he carved on the facade of the courthouse. When Mable spurned his affections, he continued carving her face but made them progressively uglier. Although this anecdote is unsubstantiated at best, Waxahachie residents don't seem to mind a bit if seeking out the distorted faces of Miss Frame is what motivates out-of-town visitors to come see one of the state's most beautiful courthouses.

TEXAS FOREST OF DWARFS

In a state that boasts more than eighty trees on the Texas A&M Forest Service's "Big Tree" list that are national champion trees, judged largely on size, is a forest of oak trees that seldom reach more than three feet in height but put down some impressive roots. These dwarf oaks, overshadowed by their big brothers on the "Big Tree" list, are the Shin oak (*Quercus Havardii*), which put down roots ninety feet into the sand—thus helping to stabilize the dunes— prompting some to theorize that the oaks are "growing in the wrong direction." These strange but true oaks may be seen in the Monahans Sandhills State Park off Interstate 20 west of Odessa, Texas.

Marble Falls, "The Blind Man's Town"

The Hill Country town of Marble Falls was founded in 1887 by Adam Rankin Johnson. Johnson had surveyed land in the area for the state in 1854. Johnson, who had attained the rank of general in the Civil War, was blinded in both eyes when shot in the face. When he returned to Texas after the war, he remembered the countryside around the falls on the Colorado River so vividly that he laid out the town site from memory with the help of his son, Robert. For years the town was known as "The Blind Man's Town."

Chicago, Texas

Originally, according to the *Handbook of Texas,* Lamesa in Dawson County was named Chicago when it was established as the county seat in 1905. When the post office was established in March of 1905, the name was changed to Lamesa from the Spanish description of the flat tableland on which it was situated.

Texas Wends Cling to Heritage

Although it no longer has a post office, the Lee County Wendish community of Serbin still clings to life. Its founding fathers' old rock Lutheran church still stands today, as well as a museum displaying evidence of the Wendish culture. Texas Wends still gather annually for the annual Serbin Homecoming Picnic. And the Wendish-German language is still spoken by some of the old-timers, both in Serbin and by others who live in the Lee County seat of Giddings, also founded by Wends. But who are these people known as Wends? They were a Slavic people referred to as a tribe by Germans. They migrated into Germany in medieval times. Some called themselves "Sorbs."

These German-speaking outsiders were persecuted by Prussian kings for hundreds of years. Their treatment became so unbearable that in 1854, in desperation, an entire Lutheran congregation numbering five hundred migrated to Texas, settling in what is today Lee County. The Wends established the community of Serbin, known as the "mother colony." The Wends established the only Wendish newspaper in the United States, the *Deutsches Volksblatt* (the "German's People's Journal").

As is often the case with many rural communities, many young Wends have long since sought lifestyles in larger cities, but Lee County's Wendish progeny have elected to cling to their heritage, although dwindling in number.

Underwater Travel in Texas

One section of a major road system in Texas is underwater 24 hours a day, 365 days a year, yet is traversed by thousands of cars and trucks daily. It is Harris County's Washburn Tunnel built in 1950. This important part of the Harris County road system goes under the Houston Ship Channel between Galena Park and the city of Pasadena. Newcomers to Houston, where daily rain is not uncommon, are sometimes startled to hear radio reporters make the tongue-in-cheek observation, "The Washburn Tunnel is underwater this morning."

FAMOUS PEOPLE IN TEXAS HISTORY

As if being from Texas isn't enough of a claim to fame, our state has its fair share of overachievers. Although you've probably read about many of these folks in history books, newspapers, and magazines, some facts have been left out of your more standard reading material because they're considered to be . . . well, trivial. As you're about to learn, sometimes the trivialities can be the most interesting parts of a person's life.

FRANCISCA ALVAREZ, "THE ANGEL OF GOLIAD"

With all of the atrocities laid at the feet of the Mexicans in Texas's struggle for independence, it is only fair that we mention some acts of benevolence by the Mexicans toward Texans. One of these involves Francisca Alvarez, known as "The Angel of Goliad," the wife of a Mexican officer under General José Urrea. When she arrived with her husband at Copano on March 27, 1836, she found Major William P. Miller with his men, who had been tied up for several hours. She ordered the cords that were restraining the Texans to be untied and refreshments be given to the prisoners. And she persuaded one of the Mexican officers to save all the prisoners he could. She personally hid several prisoners on the parapet of the fort until after the massacre. On her return to Matamoros, she also showed great kindness to Texan prisoners.

Captain James "Brit" Bailey

One early Texas settler should not go unrecognized, if only because of his strange deathbed request. Captain James "Brit" Bailey came to Texas before Stephen F. Austin and settled near the Brazoria River in what is today called Bailey's Prairie in Brazoria County. Historians say that on Bailey's deathbed he told his wife that he had "never bowed, or stooped to any man, nor had he been knocked down." He then requested that he be buried feet down, so no man could ever look upon his grave and say, "There lays old 'Brit' Bailey, flat on his back." Honoring his request, upon Bailey's death in 1833 his wife had a vertical grave dug and had Bailey's casket lowered into it feet first!

Judge Roy Bean

Some refer to the nationally renowned Judge Roy Bean, "the Law West of the Pecos," as "the hanging judge" because of his strict method of dispensing frontier justice. But it is highly unlikely that the proprietor of the Jersey Lily Saloon at Langtry, Texas, was deserving of this severe title, for he had had his own experience with the rope. He told the story of how once when he was involved with a Mexican girl, a rival strung him up to a tree. The girl succeeded in cutting him down in time to save his life, but the experience left him with a stiff neck and an aversion to this form of punishment.

In fact, according to personnel at the Judge Roy Bean visitor's center in Langtry, Texas, Judge Bean's reputation as a "hanging judge" was rubbish. As only a justice of the peace, Bean had no authority to sentence anyone to hang.

Abner "Ab" Pickens Blocker

Abner "Ab" Pickens Blocker spent his youth in ranch work and for seventeen years drove cattle up the trails from Texas to surrounding states and northward. In 1884 Blocker delivered a herd of cattle to B. H. Campbell, manager of the Capitol Syndicate's ranch in the Texas Panhandle (read about the Capitol Syndicate in the chapter "There Ought to Be a Law"). It is said that Blocker designed the brand that became the name XIT Ranch.

JIM BOWIE, HERO OF THE ALAMO . . . AND MEXICAN CITIZEN

Another Jim Bowie tale questions the very loyalty of this fallen hero of the Alamo. Bowie was actually a Mexican citizen when he fought at the Alamo, and he was married to a Mexican, two facts that shed a questionable light on Bowie's loyalty. It should be known, however, that prior to the Battle of the Alamo, when Bowie had settled in San Antonio de Bexar, Mexican law required that only citizens of Mexico could own land in Texas. As Texas land was something Bowie desperately wanted, he decided to become a citizen of Mexico. He converted to Catholicism, and with the sponsorship of his wife and his friend and business partner, Spanish governor Don Juan Martin Veramendi, Bowie's citizenship was granted on October 5, 1830. (His wife, Ursula, just happened to be Veramendi's daughter.) Despite his connections, Bowie was hailed as a great leader by Sam Houston. Conversely, he was considered a great and exceptional soldier by some Mexicans who fought under Santa Anna.

According to legend, as Mexican soldiers were gathering the Alamo defenders' bodies for cremation after the great battle was done, one Mexican officer wanted to separate Bowie's body from the rest and bury it because "Bowie's body should not be buried with the masses." (Nevertheless, his was said to have been burned with the rest of the bodies.)

JOHN NEELY BRYAN

Even though John Neely Bryan founded Dallas, there was a time, according to his own letters, when he did not feel welcome in the city. The legends of Bryan's decline claim that he left Dallas in 1849 to join the gold rush in California. It is said that Bryan was unsuccessful in finding his fortune and fell on hard times, becoming an alcoholic. His writings indicate that when he left Dallas, he left behind some enemies and generally destroyed his physical and mental health. Although it is not confirmed, it is believed that Bryan ended up in the state mental asylum where he died on September 14, 1877, and was buried in a pauper's plot in Austin, many miles away from the city he founded.

HOLLAND COFFEE

Holland Coffee was known for, among other things, establishing trading posts among the Indians in Oklahoma. His most famous post was at Preston Bend on the Texas side of the Red River, known as Coffee's Station or Coffee's Trading House. It was from this post that the town of Preston evolved. Shortly after he came to Texas, Coffee married Sophia Suttonfield Aughinbaugh, a divorcée (who later married Judge James Porter and was perhaps better known as Sophia Porter). She and Coffee built their plantation home, Glen Eden, at Preston. It was said that Coffee was a linguist, speaking fluently at least seven Indian languages.

Coffee was killed in 1846. He was entombed in a mausoleum built by his wife just a short distance from his beloved home. With the dismantling of Glen Eden in 1942 in the creation of Lake Texoma, Coffee's body was disentombed and he was interred in a cemetery near what is today the small town of Pottsboro in Grayson County.

BESSIE COLEMAN

Bessie Coleman, also known as "Queen Bess," was the first African American woman to be licensed as a pilot. Born in 1892 in Atlanta, Texas, she was introduced to airplanes as a child and knew she wanted to fly. She worked in the cotton fields of Texas and in the Chicago area in a beauty parlor. Bessie was unable to find a flying school in the United States that would accept her as a student because of her race. Hard work and a dogged determination got Bessie to France, where she learned to fly and obtained her pilot's license in 1921, two years before Amelia Earhart was licensed. "Queen Bess," the barnstormer, flew as an entertainer, doing what she loved best.

DOUGLAS "WRONG WAY" CORRIGAN

Texas-born Douglas Corrigan became internationally known as "Wrong Way" Corrigan when he took off from New York in his single-engine plane for Long Beach, California, but landed in Ireland. Corrigan was born in Galveston but moved to Los Angeles in 1922, where he became enamored with flying. He worked as an aviation mechanic and even pulled the chocks on Charles Lindbergh's *Spirit of St. Louis* on its flight from San Diego to New York before Lindbergh's pioneering solo flight across the Atlantic in 1927. By 1935, Corrigan had learned to fly and paid $310 for a secondhand 1929 Curtiss Robin monoplane that was described by friends as "a crate." Only ten people had matched Lindbergh's Atlantic crossing by that time, and Corrigan longed to join them. But the US Commerce Department rejected Corrigan's request for permission to fly the Atlantic. On July 17, 1938, Corrigan loaded 320 gallons of gasoline (enough for forty hours) into the tiny plane and took off from the East Coast's Floyd Bennet Field, pointing the nose straight east into a cloud bank even though he had announced that he was heading west to Long Beach. He forever claimed to be surprised at arriving at Ireland rather than California.

JOHN B. DENTON

The last battle in the Dallas/Fort Worth area between settlers and Indians was fought by an expedition under command of General E. H. Tarrant in what was known as the Battle of Village Creek. The battle was fought in May of 1841 where Village Creek crosses Highway 80 near present-day Arlington. One casualty of the battle was John B. Denton, for whom the city of Denton and Denton

County are named. The destruction of the village at Village Creek helped make Tarrant County safe for Anglo settlement.

DOROTHY DIX

Before Texas newspaper subscribers depended on Ann Landers or Dear Abby for their advice to the lovelorn, many newspapers, including the *Dallas Times Herald,* carried a popular columnist who dispensed her syndicated wisdom in matters of the heart. Her name was Dorothy Dix, the pen name of Elizabeth Merriwether Gilmore. Gilmore was born in Montgomery County, Tennessee, in 1870 and died in 1951. She was at one time editor of the women's department at the *New Orleans Picayune* newspaper and authored many books. She wrote her very popular column in the "golden years" of her life, which perhaps better qualified her for the sage advice she offered.

CLARA DRISCOLL, SAVIOR OF THE ALAMO

Had it not been for Clara Driscoll, we might not have an Alamo today. Born in 1881, Clara was educated in Texas and France. In 1903 she bought the Alamo to keep it from being torn down and funded extensive restoration. This earned her the title "Savior of the Alamo."

Dale Evans

Texas has produced many well-known and famous people. Dale Evans, wife of film star Roy Rogers, was born in Italy, Texas. Originally named Francis Octavia Smith, Evans made her singing debut in church at the tender age of three. In the mid-1930s, she performed as the lead singer for a band on the popular morning variety show "The Earlybirds," which was broadcast on the Dallas radio station WFAA.

John Coffee "Jack" Hays

John Coffee "Jack" Hays, commonly known as Captain Jack Hays because he was a captain in the Texas Rangers, was a surveyor by profession. He was well known as an Indian fighter and is given credit for founding the city of Oakland, California. In 1849 during the California Gold Rush, Hays led a caravan to California and for four years served as sheriff of San Francisco County. In 1853 President Franklin Pierce appointed him surveyor general of California, where he laid out the city of Oakland. Among his notable Indian fights was the defeat of the Comanche Indians from the summit of Enchanted Rock in the Texas Hill Country in the fall of 1841. Hays's last Indian fight was in Nevada in 1860. He died near Piedmont, California, in 1883.

John William Heisman

Texas and football, especially college football, seem to be inexorably linked. As more and more Texans made their way into college, the competitive spirit was kindled and the football field proved to be the dueling ground where differences were settled. With the advent of professional football and with hometowns and regions having their own franchises, partisanship was destined to flourish. Perhaps to the surprise of some, professional football, whatever the franchise, has an important link to Texas.

The most sought-after players by franchises are those college players who have won the coveted Heisman trophy. This award was named for legendary football coach John William Heisman, who was the first full-time football coach and athletic director at Rice University in Houston, Texas (1924–1927).

JAMES STEPHEN HOGG

James Stephen Hogg was the first native-born governor of Texas. He was elected governor in 1890 and retired in 1895 after serving two terms.

DOC HOLLIDAY

Dr. John H. "Doc" Holliday, the notorious gambler and gunslinger who was a friend of Wyatt Earp of Tombstone, Arizona, fame, once practiced dentistry in the city of Dallas.

SAM HOUSTON

Sam Houston, Texas's first president and the first governor, was given the name "the Raven" by the Cherokee Indians when he lived with them in Tennessee. Houston had run away from home as a teenager and lived with the Cherokee for three years, during which time he was adopted by the chief and became fluent in the Cherokee language. His adoptive father selected the name because of the "powerful medicine" of the bird in Cherokee mythology.

Sam Houston's record of public service is long, all the more impressive since it was accomplished with a minimal education. An abbreviated view of his life reveals that in 1818, after serving briefly as a teacher and then as a decorated soldier in the War of 1812, he began studying law on his own in Nashville, Tennessee. After a few months he opened a law office in Lebanon, Tennessee, and that same year was elected district attorney for the Nashville district.

He was appointed adjutant general with the rank of colonel, and in 1821 he was elected to the rank of major general. Houston was seated in the US Congress without opposition in 1823 and reelected in 1825. Two years later he became governor of Tennessee, and in 1829 Houston was granted citizenship into the Cherokee Nation and served as Indian Agent to the United States in Washington. In 1835, after moving to Texas, Houston was elected major general in the Texas army.

He was a signer of the Texas Declaration of Independence from Mexico and commander-in-chief of the Texas army. In 1836 Houston was elected president of the Republic of Texas and was reelected in 1841. He also represented Texas in the US Senate for fourteen years. Houston was also governor of Texas. Whew! All this was accomplished in spite of the fact that Houston's only formal education was a few terms in neighborhood schools.

ANDREW JACKSON HOUSTON

Andrew Jackson Houston, son of Sam Houston, was the oldest senator to serve in the US Congress when he was appointed April 21, 1941, at age eighty-seven to fill the unexpired term of Morris Shepard. Houston took the oath of office June 2, 1941, and served twenty-four days before he died in Washington, D.C., on June 26. His body was returned to Texas and buried at the San Jacinto battlefield. He served the shortest tenure of any Texan in Congress.

HOWARD HUGHES

In his great wisdom, Lord Action warned, "Power corrupts; absolute power corrupts absolutely." That idea certainly held true for a well-known Texan of the twentieth century, Howard Hughes, son of Howard R. Hughes of Houston's famed Hughes Tool Company. As scion of the wealthy Hughes fortune, young Howard used his inherited riches in what appears to be a self-serving fashion.

He did have some accomplishments of his own of which he could be justly proud. He started flying at age fourteen, and the millionaire became an accomplished aviator, having set the world land speed record for a plane (352 mph) in 1935. In 1937 he set a new transcontinental speed record (7 hours 28 minutes), and in

1938 he established a new round-the-world record (91 hours 14 minutes). In 1941 Hughes designed, built, and flew (one time) what was then the world's largest plane, known as the *Spruce Goose* because of its plywood construction. The behemoth had a wingspan of 320 feet.

Hughes evidently didn't find his aviation prowess fulfilling enough, as he later directed his attention to making motion pictures. He started in his usual Hughes modest way by purchasing the well-known RKO movie studios. Howard Hughes then proceeded to sign some of Hollywood's most luscious and voluptuous starlets, filling their pretty heads with his dreams of making them stars.

One of Hughes's big discoveries was beautiful, full-figured brunette Jane Russell. He selected this head-turner to star in a Western he was to make in 1940, *The Outlaw*. The film was to be Hughes's most famous. It starred Miss Russell and created a sensational uproar with her "romp-in-the-hay" scene. The posters and stills offered to promote the film were frowned upon by many theaters as "too risqué to post below theater marquees." As promised, the film did launch Jane Russell into her film career.

Along with his success in making motion pictures came certain eccentricities. The rich Texan developed a driving phobia about germs and disease. His phobia manifested itself by his washing and bathing several times a day. This escalated into his attempt at total isolation from germs. He disinfected his telephone constantly. Hughes did not allow even his closest associates and longtime business confidants to approach him. He touched practically no one. His eating habits were so unorthodox he was subject to illnesses, which he blamed on everything but his own eccentricities.

In his twilight years he moved, along with his meticulously selected staff (most of whom were of the Mormon faith, which he thought more trustworthy), to a Las Vegas hotel where he and his entourage occupied several floors. While there the once handsome young man with the Clark Gable mustache began to permit his personal appearance to deteriorate, letting his fingernails and toenails grow to an abnormal length. His unbarbered hair grew long and matted, as did his beard. His phobias, agitated further by numerous legal entanglements, drove the multimillionaire to become a total recluse. Photos reveal him as looking the part of a cave-dwelling hermit.

As his bizarre life drew near an end, Howard Hughes started living in hotels outside the United States. The heir to the Hughes Tool Company, whose holdings once included the RKO motion picture studios and Trans World Airlines, died a recluse, amid rumors and ridicule, on an airplane transporting the ailing millionaire from Acapulco, Mexico, to a hospital in Houston, on April 5, 1976.

ANSON JONES

Anson Jones was the last president of the Republic of Texas. He served from December 9, 1844, to February 19, 1846, when he carved a special niche for himself in Texas history by lowering the Lone Star flag of the Republic. Jones is credited with achieving annexation of Texas by the United States. In announcing the death of the Republic on February 16, 1846, at the capitol in Austin, Jones is quoted as saying,

> *The Lone Star of Texas, which ten years ago rose amid clouds over fields of carnage, obscurely seen for a while, has culminated, and following an inscrutable destiny, has passed on and become fixed forever in that constellation which all free men and lovers of freedom in the world must reverence and adore, the American union. . . . The final act in the great drama is performed. The Republic of Texas is no more!*

It has been written that as Jones lowered the flag of the Republic, its pole broke.

Scott Joplin

If you ever found yourself involuntarily tapping your toes to the ragtime piano score of the motion picture *The Sting,* then you have already been introduced to the Texan Scott Joplin. Known as the "king of ragtime," Joplin was born in Texarkana on November 24, 1868. Coming from a musical family, the young Joplin learned to improvise so well on the piano that a German musician volunteered to give him piano lessons at no cost. In his early teens Joplin was an itinerant pianist playing in the "red light" districts of Texas, Louisiana, and the Mississippi Valley. By 1885 he was playing in the "parlors" of St. Louis—the only places open to black musicians in that era—where a music called "jig piano" was in vogue. The bouncing bass line and syncopated melodic line was called "ragged-time," then simply ragtime.

Mirabeau B. Lamar

Sam Houston, after traveling five hundred miles across Texas, is quoted as declaring Texas the finest country to its extent upon the globe! This is not the voice of the freedom-fighter for which Houston is famous, but that of a visionary who saw Texas as a frontier offering much to settlers wanting to build a new life for themselves and for their progeny.

Mirabeau B. Lamar, second president of the Republic of Texas, who also distinguished himself on the field of battle, was a visionary of more poetic and grandiose fashion. History depicts

him as a little more theatrical in his pronouncements. Lamar was a man not lacking in self-confidence, as reflected by one of his war experiences at the battle of San Jacinto. Lamar successfully rode cavalier-like into the jaws of death to rescue two comrades-in-arms. This feat did not go unnoticed. As he rode out of the Mexican lines back to his own troops, the enemy acknowledged their admiration by a volley as he passed. Reining in his horse, Lamar bowed in reply.

Escapades such as these did much to feed his self-esteem. The man for whom the Mexican army offered a salute was inaugurated as the second president of the Republic on December 10 in the old capitol, which occupied the site of the present Rice Hotel, along with his vice president, David G. Burnet. An example of him as a somewhat exaggerated visionary was his dream that Texas, with successful conquests, could be an empire with its boundary extended to the Pacific Ocean.

Historians have portrayed Vice President Burnet as sharing Lamar's trait as an exaggerated visionary or dreamer. Burnet is quoted as saying, "Texas proper is bounded by the Rio Grande; but Texas as defined by the sword may comprehend the Sierra Madre. Let the sword do its proper work!"

It was no secret that Lamar and Sam Houston were opposites. There was such bad blood between them they barely escaped dueling. One of Lamar and Houston's greatest differences arose over Lamar's aggressive Indian policy, which included expulsion of the Cherokees from East Texas. Lamar's vindictive attitude toward the Indians flew in the face of Houston's personal relationship with the Cherokees, with whom he had lived and from whom he had received his Indian name, "The Raven." Lamar's expulsion of the Indians provoked new Indian depredations.

An indication of Houston's relationship with the Cherokees is the fact that Cherokee chief Bowles was wearing a sword and sash presented to him by Houston when he was shot and killed in the Battle of the Neches in July of 1839. Cherokee warriors were mobilized by Chief Bowles as a result of Lamar ordering the normally peace-loving, nonviolent tribe's expulsion from lands along the Angelina River. This was the last battle between Cherokees and whites in Texas.

Mirabeau B. Lamar was responsible for the military supply road from La Salle County to Preston Bend on the Red River. That road, which connected several military forts, today is Dallas's prestigious and beautiful business and residential artery Preston Road. It survives while the trading town of Preston Bend lies submerged under Lake Texoma. A reminder of the old trading post town is Preston Bend, a residential subdivision on the shores of Lake Texoma near the town of Pottsboro. Nearby are the graves of Holland Coffee—whose Indian trading post was the beginning of what became Preston Bend—and his widow, Sophia Porter.

Lamar eventually turned the reins of government over to his like-minded vice president, David G. Burnet. This prompted one detractor to write, in comparing Sam Houston to Lamar and Burnet, "Drunk and in a ditch, Houston is worth a thousand Lamars and Burnets."

HERMAN LEHMAN

Montechena, the "German Comanche," was born Herman Lehman on June 5, 1859, near Loyal Valley in Mason County. The son of German immigrants, he had never been to school and spoke only German when at age eleven, he and a younger brother, Willie, were captured by raiding Apaches. Willie escaped and returned home in a few days; Herman was adopted by his Apache captor and initiated into the rigors of Apache life.

He was known as Montechena and took part in expeditions against Texas Rangers, Comanches, and white settlers. After his captor was killed, he himself killed an Apache medicine man, spent a year alone on the plains, and then joined the Comanches. The "German Comanche" participated in Comanche raids and fought against the US Cavalry. He was with the last Comanche group to surrender to the US Army at Fort Sill, Oklahoma, in 1879.

He was adopted, ironically, by Quanah Parker, who undoubtedly felt a kinship with the white "Indian." Lehman was ultimately recognized as a white captive and forced to return to his Texas family, who thought him dead. He refused to conform to the white lifestyle, frequently startling his mother's guests by appearing in Indian dress. Lehman relearned German and English but never fully adjusted to white society. He died in 1932 and was buried in Loyal Valley.

THE LONE RANGER

If you grew up listening to and later watching the adventures of the "Lone Ranger" and have wondered why this defender of the rights of men and fighter for justice wears a mask, this trivia item is for you! This fictional character actually has enough of a Texas connection to fit snugly into our list of famous Texans. While our collection of Texas trivia is based on fact and well-known lore, this fragment torn from a fertile imagination has, as its basis, one of Texas's beloved icons, the Texas Rangers. Thus it warrants, we believe, special consideration and inclusion.

According to reference material enlightening us on early radio shows, in 1930 George Trindel, while searching for a radio script he could submit as a possible radio show about the Old West, invented a character based on the Texas Rangers by the name of John Reid. One of the early story lines finds Ranger Reid and his troop of five Rangers, one of which was his brother, engaged in a blazing gun-battle with the Butch Cavandish gang. The reference tells us that all the Rangers are killed save Reid, who is wounded. The lone remaining Ranger tells his Indian friend Tonto, who had nursed him back to health, "If this evil gang realizes that one Ranger survived, they would hunt him down and kill him." To this Tonto replies, "Them no think you survive, me bury five dead rangers, but make six graves."

Reid has now become the "Lone Ranger." Reid realizes the Cavandishes know him by sight and he will always be in danger. He tells Tonto that he must create a disguise or wear a mask. "Yes, that's it; I'll wear a mask." Reference material tells us that Texas Ranger Reid, now the Lone Ranger, seeks out the body of his brother, who was a member of his troop, and cuts a strip off his brother's black leather vest, from which he fashions the familiar mask. Trindel's story of the Lone Ranger and his secret, although fiction, further enhances our image of the individuals selected to make up this elite arm of our Texas criminal justice system.

MAURY AND SAMUEL A. MAVERICK

A prominent Texas family is responsible for putting two words in the dictionary. *Gobbledygook,* coined by US Representative Maury Maverick after the gobbling of turkeys, means "inflated, involved, and obscure verbiage characteristic of the pronouncements of officialdom," according to *Merriam-Webster's Collegiate Dictionary.* In a biography of the congressman, it was explained that in 1944, Maverick, while serving as chairman of the Smaller War Plants Corporations Committee, wrote a memo to his staff in which he told them to stay away from wordy, unintelligible correspondence. "Don't use so much gobbledygook." This memo was picked up by the press and printed in other publications, and the word soon became synonymous with pompous or wordy talk. Maury's grand-father, Samuel A. Maverick, a cattle owner who did not brand his calves, is responsible for giving the word *maverick* its meaning. Again referring to the dictionary, *maverick* means "an unbranded animal especially a mother's calf formerly customarily claimed by the first one branding it." A second meaning is "a refractory or recalcitrant party or group" that "initiates an independent course." It has been written that when Samuel Maverick, a signer of the Declaration of Independence, went into the cattle business before the Civil War, he branded his stock with his MK brand. He failed, however, to brand his initial herd. Thereafter, when a cowboy stumbled across an unbranded steer he considered it Maverick's, or a *maverick.*

QUINCEY MORRIS, DRACULA'S TEXAN NEMESIS

Not many people would find a connection between Jim Bowie, Alamo hero, and Dracula, befanged king of darkness. But strange as it seems, they do have something in common. In 1897 when English novelist Bram Stoker wrote his horror story about Dracula, the English were rather enamored with the wild frontier land called Texas. Stoker so loved the Texas mystique that at the end of his novel he assigned heroic Quincey Morris, portrayed as a Winchester-toting, knife-waving, gallant Texan, the bloody deed of plunging a Bowie knife into Dracula's heart, killing the "king of vampires."

CLINT MURCHESON SR.

Texans have a reputation for their wealth and for doing things in a big way. An example of this is a story about Dallas oilman Clint Murcheson Sr. It is said that Murcheson lost twelve thousand acres of land on Matagorda Island to a business associate by merely flipping a coin.

ELIZABET NEY

One of Texas's best-known artists and rather eccentric citizens was sculptress Elizabet Ney. Ney was known for her marble statues of noted Texas figures Stephen F. Austin and Sam Houston, which stand in the Texas Capitol. Duplicates were placed in Statuary Hall in the US Capitol.

According to the *Texas Almanac,* Austin, Texas, was turned on its ear by the arrival of the fifty-nine-year-old German-born sculptress in 1892. A former confidant of European nobility; she and her husband, Dr. Edmund Montgomery, had lived near Hempstead since 1873. Contrary to tradition, Ney retained her maiden name after she married Montgomery and she raised local eyebrows by doing such things as wearing bloomer-type slacks. The Montgomerys purchased the limestone plantation house Liendo in Hempstead. It was in this house that the Montgomery's two-year-old child died of diphtheria and his remains were cremated in the family's fireplace.

FRAY JUAN DE PADILLA

Fray Juan de Padilla came from Spain and traveled with Vasquez de Coronado in his expedition to find gold at Cibola. It is said that de Padilla traveled as far as Quivira, and when the main body of the expedition returned to Mexico, he and some companions decided to stay in Quivira and do some missionary work. He labored in this area for a while before deciding to push further into unexplored territory. A day's journey from Quivira the party met with hostile Indians who killed the friar. The event is believed to have taken place on November 30, 1544, and the state of Texas has recognized Padilla's martyrdom with a monument. Controversy still exists among historians, ethnologists, and archaeologists about whether Quivira was located north of the Canadian River in the Texas Panhandle or in the vicinity of present-day Wichita, Kansas.

CYNTHIA ANN PARKER

Believe it or not, the wife of a Comanche Indian chief was given land and a pension by the Texas legislature. Cynthia Ann Parker, a white child who was captured at age nine by the Comanches during a raid on Fort Parker in 1836, was raised by the Indians and later married Chief Peta Nocona. She bore him three children, one of whom, Quanah Parker, later became chief of the Comanches. Although Cynthia Ann's whereabouts were discovered several times, attempts by the whites to get her back were unsuccessful until 1860, when she was recaptured and brought to live with the whites again. Several times she tried to escape and return to the Comanche tribe for which she'd developed a love and loyalty. In 1861 the state legislature granted her a pension of $100 a year for five years and a league of land to be administered by a guardian.

Lucy Holcomb Pickens

It could be said that Lucy Holcomb Pickens had the look of money. The daughter of Beverly Holcomb of Marshall, Lucy married Colonel Francis Pickens, who was later elected governor of South Carolina. As first lady of the state, and for her support of the Confederate army, Lucy was known as "Lady Lucy, Queen of the Confederacy," and her picture graced the Confederate currency.

Bill Pickett's Bulldog Grip

Bill Pickett, inventor of steer wrestling, or "bulldogging," was born in Liberty Hill, Texas, of black and Choctaw Indian descent. He was a range rider and did odd jobs on various ranches. Once while loading cattle into a stock car, he was confronted by a runaway steer. He took the steer by the horns, twisted its neck, and bit into its lip, holding on like a bulldog until the steer fell to the ground. He developed this technique into an act, and in Fort Worth in the 1900s he joined the Miller Brothers' Wild West show. The act was so effective that he was credited with inventing the art of steer wrestling, or "bulldogging" as it was known. Pickett's favorite horse bore the unusual name of Spradley.

C. W. Post

Although C. W. Post was not born in Texas, the inventor of Post Toasties and other breakfast cereals as well as the drink Postum literally made his mark on the state's map. He made his home in Texas in the 1880s and founded the city of Post in Garza County.

Wiley Post

Wiley Post, born in Grand Saline, Texas, lost an eye in an oil field accident yet was an accomplished flier. He and his friend Will Rogers attempted a flight to Siberia in Post's plane, the *Winnie Mae*, in August 1935, when their plane was forced down due to engine trouble near an Eskimo village in Alaska. After repairing the engine, the two attempted to take off, but the plane crashed and both Post and Rogers were killed.

Harriet Potter

Since 1998, a Texas granite marker partially funded by a local funeral home has been the only marker recognizing the Texas pioneer woman who may well have set the standard by which common-law marriages became accepted in Texas. The simple marker bearing the inscription "To honor and remember Harriet Potter Ames bravest woman in Texas" stands on a little plot of East Texas soil near her Caddo Lake home.

Although her burial place is not known, this woman has earned a place in the pages of Texas history. Much of what is known of this pioneer Texas woman is found in her autobiography, written during the final days of her life at age eighty-three while she was living with her daughter in New Orleans. What is known is that she lived in Texas during some of its most tumultuous years!

Born in New York in 1810, Harriet Ann Moore's life runs parallel to the birth of Texas. Harriet married Solomon Page, who fought in the Texas War of Independence. Page stranded his wife and two children on the South Texas prairie, where she found herself caught up in the famous "Runaway Scrape," the hysterical flight of Texas residents fleeing their homes ahead of what they thought was Santa Anna's army. Harriet, thinking her husband had been killed in the Battle of San Jacinto, took up with her rescuer, Robert Potter, a signer of the Texas Declaration of Independence, and for whom Potter County was to be named.

In her memoirs Harriet said her marriage to Potter had been by bond, "an agreement signed before witnesses." The freedom fighter and his wife lived together for seven years. They considered their marriage acceptable as common-law marriage. They moved to land Potter had been granted for his military service. The property on Caddo Lake was called "Potter's Point."

In 1842 Potter was rousted out of bed and shot in the head while trying to escape enemies he had made while involved in the East Texas "Regulator-Moderator War." This was a little-known rebellion against the Republic of Texas. Following Robert's cruel death, Harriet tried to inherit Potter's land. She was unable to do so because it was held that she and Potter were not legally married. Harriet Potter's fruitless court battle to prove herself Potter's legal wife was the foundation for today's laws that recognize common-law marriage, according to historians.

ANN SHERIDAN

Ann Sheridan, the film actress, was born February 21, 1915, in Denton. Christened Clara Lou Sheridan, for a brief time she attended North Texas State Teacher's College, now the University of North Texas. In 1933 she was one of thirty-three young women chosen to promote a Paramount film by taking part in a beauty contest. She won a screen contract, and her first five pictures were Westerns. Publicity releases soon billed her as the "Oomph Girl" of the movies. In 1939 she was contracted by Warner Brothers and soon reached stardom.

Willie Shoemaker

One of horse racing's best-known and winningest jockeys, Willie Shoemaker, was born in the El Paso County border town of Fabens. He raced more than forty thousand horses and was the oldest jockey (at fifty-four) to win the Kentucky Derby, which also was his fourth time to win that race.

Charles A. Siringo

Charles A. Siringo was born February 7, 1855, in Matagorda County, Texas. After several trips on the Mississippi from New Orleans to St. Louis and back, he was employed as a cowboy and became a trail driver on the Chisolm Trail in 1876. He worked as a cowpuncher for fifteen years, working on several large ranches on the New Mexico border. After serving as a Pinkerton detective throughout the West for twenty-two years, he became a storekeeper in Kansas, where he wrote several books. He died in Hollywood, California, in 1928.

Erastus "Deaf" Smith

Deaf Smith County itself was named for one of the heroes of the Texas Revolution, Erastus "Deaf" Smith. Smith was born in New York, but his family moved to Mississippi and later Texas, where he made his home in 1821. He moved around trying to improve his health but never overcame his deafness. Smith married a Mexican woman and was neutral when the Texans started their move toward independence from Mexico, but his neutrality ended over a personal dispute with the Mexicans: Smith went to San Antonio to visit his family but was refused admittance and, as a result, decided to join the Texans. He was well known as a scout and his services were accepted when he volunteered. Smith served loyally throughout the battles for independence and is considered by some as a little-known hero of the Texas Revolution—he is given credit for destroying Vince's bridge before the Battle of San Jacinto, which prevented reinforcements from aiding Santa

Anna's army. This may have easily been Deaf Smith's most valuable effort on the Texans' behalf. He died in Richmond, Texas, on November 30, 1837, at the age of fifty.

JAMIE STEWART
An Austin woman, Jamie Stewart, made her mark in the world sports records in 1976 by being the first Texas woman to swim the twenty-one-mile English Channel. She made the crossing in fourteen and a half hours.

SAMUEL HAMILTON WALKER
Although Samuel Hamilton Walker was born in Maryland, he made a name for himself as a true "man of the West." After distinguishing himself as an Indian fighter in Georgia and Florida, he came to Texas in 1836 and joined the Ranger company of the well-known Captain John C. Hays, where, according to *The New Handbook of Texas,* he distinguished himself as a fighter with "courage and coolness." About 1849 he was sent to New York to deal with Samuel Colt regarding the purchase of arms for the Republic of Texas. He found Colt and made certain suggestions for changes of the popular "Texas" model revolver and was largely responsible for the successfully modified pistol, known thereafter as the "Walker Colt." After participating in the Mier Expedition, which resulted in his capture by the Mexicans (see Black Bean Death Warrant in chapter 7, "Lone Star War Stories"), Walker fought with General Zachary Taylor in the Mexican-American War. Walker was killed while leading a charge upon Huamantla. He was buried in San Antonio.

WILLIAM "BIGFOOT" WALLACE
William Alexander Anderson Wallace was born in Virginia in 1817. It is said that as a Scotsman, his clan was strong in him. We owe his family ties for his being a minor but colorful part of our Texas heritage. When he learned that a brother and a cousin had

been shot down in the Goliad Massacre, he set out for Texas "to take pay out of the Mexicans." He later said that the account had been squared.

Wallace stood six feet two inches in his moccasins and weighed 240 pounds. His size, no doubt, accounted for his descriptive nickname. Wallace quit farming in La Grange in 1840 and moved to Austin. He claimed to have seen the last buffalo in the region run down Congress Avenue. When Wallace decided there were too many people in Austin, he moved to San Antonio.

"Bigfoot" volunteered for the ill-fated Mier Expedition, which landed him in the notorious Perote Prison in the Mexican state of Vera Cruz. Following his release from Perote, he joined John Coffee "Jack" Hays's company of the Texas Rangers. He served with the Rangers in the Mexican War. In the 1850s, as a captain, he commanded a Ranger company of his own, fighting border bandits as well as Indians.

Wallace drove a mail hack from San Antonio to El Paso. On one occasion, after losing his mules to Indians, he walked to El Paso, and it is said he ate twenty-seven eggs at the first house he came to before continuing on into town for a full meal. The last years of his life were spent in Frio County near a small village named Bigfoot. It is said that Wallace was an avid storyteller with a tendency to "stretch the blanket" or embroider the details.

"THREE-LEGGED WILLIE" WILLIAMSON

There are many legends about one of Texas's most illustrious characters and an early proponent of Texas independence, Robert McAlpin "Three-Legged Willie" Williamson. One that writers say most probably depicts Williamson's character is the legend of the case of "Colt vs. Bowie."

Williamson was born in Georgia in 1804. When he was fifteen, his schooling was terminated by an illness, which left him a cripple for life. His right leg was drawn back at the knee;

the wooden leg he wore from the knee to the ground resulted in his nickname of "Three-Legged Willie." Williamson read much during his illness and was admitted to the bar before he was nineteen. He practiced law in Georgia for more than a year and then migrated to Texas in 1829.

In Texas, he edited a newspaper for a short time and made an appeal for Texas to resist the Mexican tyranny. He was sent to the "Consultation" as a representative, and the government commissioned him a major in 1835 to organize a Ranger company. As a Ranger, he participated in the Battle of San Jacinto.

In 1836 the first Congress elected him judge of the third judicial district, and he went on to have a long and eventful political career. His district included Shelby County, where court had never been held. When locals heard that court would be held, they got up a resolution against it. Legend goes that when presented with it, Judge Williamson asked, "By whose authority was such a resolution presented?" And the presenter, who like others in Shelby County lived by the "law of the Bowie," took out his knife of the same name and laid it across the document, claiming, "This is the law in this county!" "Three-Legged Willie" unholstered his Colt and laid it across the Bowie knife, announcing, "And this is the Constitution that overrides the law. Call the court to order!"

BOB WILLS

Bob Wills, the legendary country-and-western fiddler and swing band leader, was born in 1905 in the Limestone County town of Kosse. He lived for a while in Turkey, Texas, where it is said he made his first solo appearance playing the fiddle at age ten. Wills quit his barbering job in Turkey to go to Fort Worth to pursue his entertainment career. Bob Wills became popular as the fiddling leader of the western swing band "Bob Wills and the Texas Playboys." The Bob Wills Museum is at Turkey, where each year the town holds a "Bob Wills Day."

GENERAL WILLIAM JENKINS WORTH

General William Jenkins Worth, for whom the city of Fort Worth was named, is buried beneath a monument on the corner of Fifth Avenue and Broadway in New York City. Worth, a New York native, served in the War of 1812. Although not a graduate of the academy, he served as commandant of West Point Military Academy from 1820 to 1828. He served in the Mexican War under both Zachary Taylor and Winfield Scott and was brevetted as a brigadier general for service in the Seminole War. Worth was ordered to Texas in 1848 and died there in 1849. He was returned to his native state for burial. The military establishment, Fort Worth, and the city that grew from it were named for him.

BABE DIDRIKSON ZAHARIAS

One of America's best-known and most versatile athletes, Babe Didrikson Zaharias was born Mildred Ella Didrikson in Port Arthur, Texas, on June 26, 1914. She attended school in Beau-

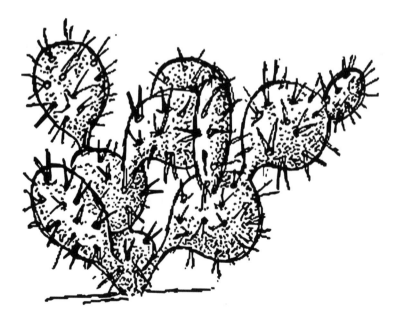

mont, then in 1930 moved to Dallas, where she started her track and field career. The three-time basketball all-American, Olympic gold medalist, and world-class golfer was named by the Associated Press as Woman Athlete of the Year six times. Babe got her nickname as a young girl because of her unusual athletic ability at a time when Babe Ruth was the best-known athlete in America. She became a professional and went into show business for a short time, singing and playing the harmonica. In 1953 Babe underwent an operation for cancer, and few believed she would return to sports; however, she came back to win several professional golf tournaments, including the National Open. Her career was cut short when she died of cancer in 1956 at the age of forty-two. She was buried in Beaumont, which is now the home of the Babe Didrikson Zaharias Museum.

TEXAS RANGERS

It's impossible to write much about Texans without mentioning the Texas Rangers. These distinctive peace officers are known and respected far and wide and considered by many as the ultimate lawmen. Their motto, "One riot, one Ranger," is almost as legendary as "Remember the Alamo." The Texas Rangers is the oldest force of its kind in the world, but exactly when the group originated is difficult to pinpoint. In 1823 Stephen F. Austin employed ten men to serve as "Rangers," but there is no record of their operation. Again in 1826 Austin called a meeting of the representatives of the six militia districts, and it was agreed to keep twenty to thirty Rangers in service at all times. It was not until the Texas Revolution began in 1835 that the force was given legal status, when it was realized that if war came with Mexico, the danger of incursions from the west would be increased and that some provision should be made to protect that quarter. On October 17, 1835, Daniel Parker offered a resolution creating a Corps of Texas Rangers consisting of small detachments stationed on the Indian frontier. Other historians say that the Rangers were first organized on November 26, 1835, when R. M. "Three-Legged Willie" Williamson was commissioned a major and ordered to organize a corps of Rangers to guard the frontier from Indian attacks.

As peace officers, the Texas Rangers' commission is different from other law officers because they are authorized to operate throughout the state. They have never worn a prescribed uniform. Their primary function has been one of maintaining or restoring order in situations that get beyond control of local officers but are not serious enough to justify the use of military force. The Rangers have protected Texans not only from Mexican and Indian raiders in the early days but also from outlaw bands, feudists, stock thieves, and local rioters in later years.

CHIEF YELLOW BEAR

Based on a portion of the book *How Fort Worth Became the Texas-Most City*, one is compelled to believe that the American Indians were practically destined to be totally overcome at the hands of the white man. This book tells us that on December 19, 1875, Comanche Chief Yellow Bear and his nephew, Quanah Parker, checked into the Pickwick Hotel in Fort Worth, which proudly boasted of "artificial gas lights." But this "white man's magic" claimed the life of Chief Yellow Bear. It seems that when the two chiefs turned out the gas lights, they didn't close the valve all the way. After they rolled out their blankets to sleep, Yellow Bear was asphyxiated by the fumes.

THE CRIMINAL ELEMENT

ALTHOUGH TEXAS CAN BOAST IT IS HOME TO PLENTY OF FAMOUS Americans, from war heroes and movie stars to inventors and our own iconic Texas Rangers, it's also seen its fair share of train robbers, highwaymen, hucksters, and desperados—but on a larger scale than in some other places, some may argue. Maybe it's because this great state was born with battle scars on its face; maybe because ours is the kind of place that produces unusually tough characters; or maybe it's just easy for a no-account on the run from the law to find a remote place to lie low for a good long while. Regardless of how these folks got here, the stories they left behind can make for some awfully interesting reading.

FARMER FELONS

Although they may not know it or even care, many convicted felons in Southeast Texas can blame the Civil War for their places of confinement and type of labor. According to the *Handbook of Texas,* agriculture was the economic foundation of Brazoria County in its early days. Sugar and cotton plantations along the rivers and deeper creeks flourished during the antebellum period in Texas, making Brazoria the wealthiest county in the state. With abolition and the freeing of slaves, however, agriculture declined sharply in this region, and many of the plantations were broken into small farms and turned into pasture land. Other land parcels became the Ramsey, Clemens, and Darrington prison farms of the Texas Department of Corrections. Agricultural efforts on this land still exist but are now performed not under the watchful eye of the master's overseer but instead under the eye of an armed guard whose job is to help the laborer learn that "crime doesn't pay."

MONROE EDWARDS

One of Texas's earliest and more able criminals was Monroe Edwards. Edwards came to Texas from Kentucky in 1827 and became involved in smuggling slaves from Cuba to Texas. His first venture brought him some $50,000, with which he bought land in Brazoria County, which he called Chenengo Plantation. Life on the plantation was not exciting enough for Edwards, however, and in partnership with one Christopher Dart, he continued in slave smuggling. After several masterful swindles on the East Coast that spanned the Atlantic to Europe, Edwards was apprehended in Philadelphia and tried in New York where he was sentenced to Sing Sing Prison. Ironically enough, he died in 1847 after being severely whipped by prison authorities for attempting to escape.

THOMAS JEFFERSON RUSK

The pursuit of thieves gave Texas one of her most illustrious personages. Thomas Jefferson Rusk left Georgia in pursuit of his business partners, who had absconded with his money and fled to Texas. Rusk settled in Texas, and in 1835 he organized a company of volunteers from Nacogdoches and joined the Texas Revolution. He became inspector general for the army. Rusk was a signer of the Texas Declaration of Independence. He was elected secretary of war in March 1836 and later elected chief justice of the Texas Supreme Court. Rusk used his influence to get Texas annexed into the United States, and he, along with Sam Houston, was elected to the US Senate. In 1856 he was considered a political candidate for US president. After his wife died in 1856, Rusk became despondent and committed suicide at his home in 1857. Rusk County is named for him.

FIRST WOMAN HANGED IN TEXAS

The story of Chapita (some say Chepita) Rodriguez, who was executed for an alleged murder, is a mix of fact and legends of the Rio Grande Valley. The name Chapita is a diminutive form of Chepa, the nickname for Josefa. Chapita lived in a hut on the Welder ranch lands on the Arkansas River. San Patricio County records show that in August of 1863 Chapita and Juan Silvera were indicted for murdering a horse trader named John Savage. His body was found in the Arkansas River near Chapita's cabin. When the court met at the town of San Patricio, then the county seat, Juan Silvera was convicted of second-degree murder and given a five-year prison sentence. Chapita was found guilty of first-degree murder and sentenced by Judge Benjamin Neal to be hanged. Mercy was recommended because her conviction was based largely on circumstantial evidence. Nevertheless Judge Neal ordered the sentence to be carried out, and on November 13, 1863, Chapita was hanged from a mesquite tree in the Nueces River bottoms near San Patricio and buried in an unmarked grave.

It was later rumored that Chapita's long-lost son was the one who murdered Savage. Another story is that a dying man confessed to the murder. Whatever the truth might have been, Chapita's guilt remains questionable. Legend has it that Chapita's ghost roams the riverbanks where she was hanged. Some even believe there is a curse on the village of San Patricio that brought about its decline—it lost its position as county seat to Sinton in 1893.

CLAY ALLISON

Clay Allison, renowned Texas rancher and gunfighter, was known as "Clay Allison of the Washita." In the 1870s he appeared in Colfax County, New Mexico, allegedly after fighting an unusual duel in a roomy grave dug by his opponent and him. The winner was supposed to shovel dirt over the loser. Allison did the shoveling. Maurice Fulton, in a book about Allison, writes that after a life of lead-slinging against such notables as Bat Masterson and Wyatt

Earp, Allison met his death when he fell from a loaded wagon and was crushed beneath its wheels.

Sam Bass's Last Ride

Stagecoaches and trains were popular targets for bandits such as Sam Bass. From Indiana originally, Bass worked as a teamster around Denton. He went north to Nebraska with a cattle drive and fell in with a group of outlaws. After they held up a Union-Pacific train in the fall of 1877, Bass returned to North Texas. He planned to rob a bank in Round Rock, near Austin, in 1878, but one of the gang members alerted the Texas Rangers. When the Bass gang rode into Round Rock on July 19, Rangers confronted them, and Bass was mortally wounded in the fray.

Who Is Buried in Sam Bass's Grave?

There are some who believe the legendary outlaw's remains are buried not at Round Rock but elsewhere in Texas. This theory maintains that Sam Bass survived the ambush at Round Rock and managed to make it to the town of Grapevine in Tarrant County before his wounds did him in.

According to Grapevine mayor Bill Tate, who is well versed in Bass lore, Bass had family living in Grapevine. Tate remembers as a child going with his father to hoe graves at local cemeteries. At the Old Hall Cemetery in Lewisville in Denton County, he remembers seeing a marker engraved "Sam Bass." Although that could have been for another deceased man of the same name, it

nevertheless piqued Tate's interest in the legendary Bass's fate. According to a book published by the Grapevine Historical Society, *Grapevine Area History,* Bass was buried in a cemetery near Grapevine. Billie Sparger, who says Bass was her great-grandfather James A. Hensley's brother-in-law, gives this account in the book:

> *Several of the gang were killed that day. Sam, himself, was mortally wounded. The sheriff picked up one young man, yelling, "I shot Sam Bass!" They hauled the dead man through the town yelling all the way, "Sam Bass is dead, come see Sam Bass!" They buried the poor man in the Round Rock Cemetery. Even today people come from all over to see his grave.*
>
> *[Nevertheless] Sam, though badly wounded, managed to make it to the railroad tracks not far away. . . . The story goes that when he got to Grapevine, Sam was, indeed, dead. The man at the depot knew James Hensley. He sent a man to tell him to come about Sam. According to Grandpa Hensley, when he got there, the main man at the depot had Sam dressed, wrapped in a blanket, and placed in a pine box. Grandpa paid him and told him, "Keep quiet about this." Grandpa Hensley did a lot of business there and knew he could trust him. James Hensley and two black men at the ranch, Dad Nelson and another man, placed Sam on a wagon and buried him by lantern light, in a secret place, where he could rest in peace.*

Elsewhere in the book it is mentioned that "Bass was buried during the night at Parker Memorial Cemetery near the Hensley family plot."

BEN THOMPSON

Born in 1843 in England, Thompson reflected a violent streak at an early age. His family moved to Austin, Texas, when he was a child. When Ben was a mere thirteen years old, he deliberately shot and wounded a playmate. He was tried but not imprisoned.

His violent side showed itself again in New Orleans when he killed a man in a knife duel. After escaping New Orleans he returned to Austin.

When the Civil War broke out, fighting for the Confederates gave rise to other crimes of personal violence. Thompson went to Mexico to fight for Maximilian I. After returning to Austin, a murder there led to a prison term. Later in Austin, Thompson became city marshal. Ironically, his skill with a gun made him effective in reducing the crime rate in that city.

In San Antonio Thompson got into an argument with the owner of a vaudeville theater and shot the man dead. He was once again tried and acquitted. But the case was far from being concluded: Two years later Thompson and another lawman of ill repute, John King Fisher, returned to the theater where both men died in a fusillade of bullets fired by friends of the murdered theater owner. The assassins had effectively rid the state of two of its tarnished badges.

THE JAIL THAT BILLY THE KID BROKE INTO

Although there are, for obvious reasons, precious few remaining newspaper accounts and no eyewitnesses to interview about the many exploits of the young man known to us today as Billy the Kid, volumes have been written based upon the legends left behind by his contemporaries. One of his chroniclers was his nemesis, Sheriff Pat Garrett. Many of these legends are based upon facts as remembered by those who lived in those headline-making days of the desperado who, it is said, killed twenty-one men before he was twenty-one years of age. Aficionados of Wild West outlaws remember his bloody escape from the Lincoln County, New Mexico, jail, early in the afternoon of April 28, 1881, when he shot and killed two of Pat Garrett's best guns, J. W. Bell and Bob Olinger, after being shackled hand and foot and placed in a second-floor cell. But little has been written about the Kid's only recorded incident where he broke *into* jail, which just happened to be in Texas.

The incident is recorded in *Pat F. Garrett's Authentic Life of Billy the Kid,* which was published in 1927.

The story of Billy the Kid's break-in of the El Paso County jail is truly a piece of Texas lore that is backed up by the Texas State Historical Association. To set the scene we must remind you that the small Mexican pueblo of San Elizario was El Paso's county seat from the time the county was established in 1850 until 1876. Around 1850 El Paso's first county jail was built. After "the Kid" had killed his second man, he became a fugitive in Old Mexico.

While there he formed an alliance with Melquides Segura and Jesse Evans. After returning to New Mexico, Billy the Kid learned that his friend and partner in crime Segura had run afoul of the law and had been arrested in San Elizario and placed in jail there. The Kid learned that Segura might be in danger in that town. He decided to go to San Elizario and free Segura from custody.

According to Garrett's story, it was in the fall of 1876 that the Kid made the eighty-one-mile ride to the Rio Grande town. Traveling along the Rio Grande, he stopped briefly in El Paso, known then as Franklin, Texas. Upon arrival at the little San Elizario jail, he aroused the Mexican who was standing guard at the lock-up. He tricked the guard into opening the door "for some additional prisoners." He then grabbed the jailer's arm, and with the barrel of his revolver acting as a persuader, he convinced the guard to surrender his handgun and the keys to the jail. He and Segura shackled the two guards on duty to a post outside. They then locked the jail with its new prisoners and rode into the night!

Today, the Old El Paso County Jail is a museum dedicated to preserving the site as the only jail Billy the Kid broke *into.* Operated by the San Elizario Genealogical and Historical Society, the museum is open six days a week, with free admission—so you don't need to get past a guard to get in anymore!

JOHN KING FISHER, FLAMBOYANT GUNFIGHTER

He was described as wearing an ornamented Mexican sombrero, a black Mexican jacket embroidered with gold, a crimson sash and boots, and tiger skin chaps, along with a brace of silver-plated ivory-handled revolvers. This man of violence was a native of Kentucky. Following the death of his father, he cut his teeth on violence when he was employed by a justice of the peace to discourage rustling activities.

This renegade lawman worked just long enough in this capacity to learn how profitable this criminal venture could be. He then started rustling stock for himself. During the 1870s he was the scourge of the Rio Grande border. This criminal activity led to considerable violence. Fisher was arrested several times by Texas Rangers and is reported to have been charged with eleven murders but never convicted.

Having a "clean" record, Fisher was appointed deputy sheriff of Uvalde County in 1883. It is written that in Fisher's territory he was respected and feared. A certain road branch bore the sign "This is King Fisher's road. Take the other!"—advice that seldom went unheeded. The gaudily dressed gunslinger was assassinated with Ben Thompson in a San Antonio vaudeville theater on March 11, 1884.

BELLE STARR

An interesting bit of trivia is about a Texan who held the title of Queen. It was a dubious honor, for the exact title as recorded by historians was "Outlaw Queen of the Indian Territory." Belle Starr was born Myrabelle Shirley in 1848 in Missouri. At the end of the Civil War, her family moved to Scyene, Texas, and settled on a farm in the community east of Dallas. She eloped with a horse thief, Jim Reed of Missouri. Reed, who was also a stage-coach bandit, was wanted in connection with several killings. He was killed resisting arrest in August of 1874. During the next few years, his widow did some roving around and was accused of disposing of livestock stolen by her male friends. In 1880 she went to the Indian Territory and married a Cherokee Indian by the name of Sam Starr, and their place became headquarters for a band of ruffians. In February of 1883 both Sam and Belle were convicted of horse theft and sent to prison. Belle was killed by an unknown gunman on a road near her home in 1889.

JOHN WESLEY HARDIN

Life did not reflect well on John Wesley Hardin. One of Texas's most notorious outlaws, Hardin met his end when a constable mistook his reflection in the mirror as Hardin coming after him. Constable John Selman shot Hardin in the back of the head as he sat in the Acme Saloon on August 19, 1895. The outlaw boasted nearly thirty notches on his gun, and although he tried to stay out of trouble, he constantly ran afoul of the law. Historians say, however, that Hardin was in El Paso that particular time to act as an attorney for a relative.

PILOT KNOB

A hand-drawn map of early Denton County settlements included an unusual land formation on the North Texas blackland prairie. Identified on the map as Pilot Knob, it was noteworthy not only because of its topography but also because of its interest to aficionados of Texas outlaws. The nine-hundred-foot knob of earth located about four miles from the city of Denton was supposedly a hangout for stage, train, and bank robber Sam Bass. Wayne Gard, in his biography of Sam Bass, alluded to Bass's use of Pilot Knob. In one reference Gard reported that Bass, while on the run from a posse, stopped at a farm at Pilot Knob to buy provisions. He also indicated that Bass used the high point on the North Texas prairie as a lookout. The person who drew the map also referred to the Knob as a "rendezvous point for Sam Bass," and he and his gang supposedly hid in a cave there. Based on facts pointed out in Robert Nash's book *Bloodletters and Badmen,* Bass and his gang may have been hiding out at the Knob when they planned their ill-fated attempt at robbing the bank at Round Rock near Austin, Texas, in which Bass was mortally wounded on July 19, 1878.

JOHN SELMAN

Another product of the lawlessness of Texas at the close of the nineteenth century was ironically best remembered as the slayer of badman John Wesley Hardin. John Selman was born in Shackelford County near old Fort Griffin. After ranching in the area, Selman in 1876 became a deputy sheriff under John M. Larn, where he was involved in breaking up cattle and horse theft rings. He was, according to a later confession, involved in an extra-legal vigilance committee that lynched a number of thieves. In 1877 Larn got a contract to supply beef to the army posts at Fort Griffin. Soon there was talk about him and Selman butchering stolen cattle. In June 1878 Larn was arrested, but Selman escaped to West Texas, where his cattle rustling career continued. He was later recognized while traveling under another name and

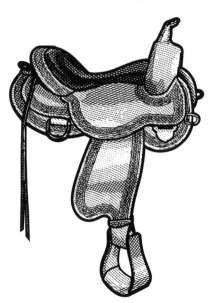

was arrested. The Texas Rangers brought him back to Shackelford County. While under indictment he was allowed to escape.

Despite his several brushes with the law, in 1882 Selman turned up in El Paso serving as a peace officer once again. Selman's claim to historic fame was also his undoing. In 1895 Selman, hearing that the infamous gunslinger John Wesley Hardin had threatened him, walked into the Acme Saloon where Hardin was gambling. The constable with the tarnished badge placed two neat holes in the back of Hardin's evil head. Selman claimed that Hardin had seen his reflection in the mirror behind the bar and had attempted to draw on him and that he shot in self-defense. He was acquitted, but the following year, on April 6, 1896, he was killed by a deputy US marshal.

Frank James: Infamous Outlaw, Shoe Salesman

Alexander Franklin James, brother to Jesse James and part of the bank robbing, murdering James gang, strange as it seems, had a legitimate job as a shoe salesman at Dallas's Sanger Brothers department store. A manuscript written by a fellow worker indicates that Frank James, whom he described as "friendly and generous," was working in the Dallas store in the latter 1880s.

James surrendered to Governor Crittenden on October 5, 1882, and confessed that he was tired of being on the run. The Missouri governor, after promising James protection, had the outlaw jailed to await trial on several robbery and murder charges. After his acquittal, Frank James was freed and returned to his farm. He lived there until he died on February 18, 1915.

The First *Rolling Stone*

The rock 'n' roll magazine *Rolling Stone* is a not a new name to Texans—a magazine named *Rolling Stone* was published in Austin, Texas, between 1894 and 1895. It contained humorous articles, political notes, cartoons, and jokes and was published by Sydney Porter, who came to Texas from North Carolina. Porter went on to bigger fame writing under the pseudonym of O. Henry but was later charged with embezzlement from a bank where he had worked as a teller. He fled to Central America; in 1897 he returned from Honduras to visit his sick wife and was arrested in March 1898. He was found guilty and sentenced to the federal penitentiary in Columbus, Ohio. It was there that Porter began writing short stories, many of which had Texas settings.

WILLIAM MARSH RICE MURDERED FOR HIS FORTUNE

Although many Texans may be able to tell you that the estate of William Marsh Rice was used to establish Rice Institute (now Rice University) in Houston, few might know the circumstances surrounding the death of one of Texas's most noted benefactors. On September 23, 1900, Rice died in New York at age eighty-five of what were supposedly natural causes, but investigation revealed that he was murdered by his valet, Charles F. Jones, and an attorney, Albert Patrick, who was allegedly interested in Mr. Rice's estate. While it is doubtful many students at Rice know this story, it's even less well known that Mr. Rice's ashes are buried under the statue of him on the Rice campus.

VANITY TRIPS UP "WILD BUNCH"

While being pursued by law posses as well as being dogged by the Pinkerton Detective Agency, Wild West outlaws Robert Leroy Parker and Harry Longabaugh—better known as Butch Cassidy and the Sundance Kid—along with others who made up the bank and train robbing gang known variously as "The Hole-in-the-Wall Gang" and the "Wild Bunch," headed for Fort Worth, Texas, where they holed up at Fannie Porter's brothel. The year was 1901.

While laying low in the bustling cow town, patronizing such places as the White Elephant Saloon, they strolled the town's street and took in its pleasures. One day they passed a photographer's studio, and feeling pretty cocky, no doubt, they had a group portrait made. The photographer was so proud of his handiwork that he posted a copy of the photo in his window as an example of his fine work. This led to the undoing of the notorious gang. A Pinkerton detective strolling the streets of Fort Worth noticed the photo, and after learning more about its time frame, alerted local lawmen to the presence of the "Wild Bunch" in their fair city.

The subsequent flurry of excitement resulted in the much-sought-after gang's flight into a questionable future! While some hold that the gang fled to South America, where they were killed by local police, others claim that Cassidy, at least, returned to his place of birth in the western United States, where he lived out the remainder of his life.

A reminder of the presence of this infamous gang of outlaws is today's very modern business development in downtown Fort Worth, "Sundance Square." Ed Bass, its developer, had these historic exploits in mind when he named the new development.

John Wilkes Booth

A saloon-keeper in Granbury, before his death in 1903, made an astonishing admission: he was President Lincoln's assassin, John Wilkes Booth. According to a story in the July 28, 1978, edition of the *Dallas Times Herald*, residents believed the claim of John St. Helen, who had moved to Granbury five years earlier and frequently quoted Shakespeare. Booth had been a noted Shakespearean actor. After his death St. Helen's body was mummified and exhibited in traveling circuses. Adding to the mystery, the body reportedly disappeared in 1938.

Grapevine's "Cross-Bar Hotel"

If you want to see how attitudes have changed about law-breakers in Texas, it is not necessary to visit the state's numerous "hanging trees" that were associated with the lawlessness of the Old West. All one has to do is visit the beautiful, history-packed Tarrant County city of Grapevine, Texas. There, sitting on the northern fringes of the DFW Airport, one can inspect low-budget housing for those who ran afoul of the law in the early twentieth century. Standing on the city's historic Main Street as a warning beacon for all to see and as a concrete (literally) "word to the wise" is the Grapevine Calaboose, which, incidentally, comes from the Spanish slang word for jail, "calabozo."

According to the Grapevine Historical Foundation, in 1909 the Grapevine town council voted unanimously to build the community's first calaboose-town jail. Grapevine had previously relied on the Tarrant County sheriff to provide law enforcement. Founded in the 1850s, the town would now have its own lawman and jail. The council gave town marshal W. T. Bigbee authorization to construct the 8-foot by 100-foot by 8-foot concrete jail. In the same meeting, Marshal Bigbee was given $4.50 for the purchase of a pair of handcuffs. "It is supposed the marshal had his own gun." The marshal was offered $25 a month.

If its cramped size is not enough to be convincing of the locals' attitude toward wayward citizens and visitors, perhaps its accommodations will show how bereft of comfort it was. The calaboose, which was, no doubt, home to numerous rowdy cowboys in its day, was outfitted with a single iron cot, and a tarp covered its openings to keep out chilly winds. Eventually these accommodations became inadequate to house even the occasional inebriated citizen and fell into ruin. It was not used much after 1953 to hold prisoners and was moved to the city's historic district to sit along with the city's other buildings of yesteryear.

Vigilantism in 1910 Dallas

I was a deputy sheriff for Dallas County in the 1950s when I first heard vague stories about a black man being hanged from a second-story window of Dallas's "old red" courthouse across the street from the sheriff's office. It was not until forty years later that I heard the full story of this un-Dallas-like family secret. The full story is the exact reason we keep our family secrets hidden like skeletons in a closet: They are ugly!

It is to be remembered that at this time Dallas was home to Ku Klux Klan Chapter 66, the largest in the country. Among its members were "pillars of the community" such as lawyers, judges, policemen, and other prominent citizens. The Klan's strength is underscored by the fact that in 1922 a prominent Dallas dentist was elected Grand Wizard of the Klan.

The 1910 mob lynching I was told about involved a sixty-eight-year-old black man, Allen Brooks, who was accused of raping a three-year-old white girl. It was alleged that Brooks was found in a barn with the girl; who was reported as missing. Brooks was to have been tried for the alleged offense, when a lynch-mob mentality took over. According to reports, the vigilantes knew they could find Brooks at his trial in the Dallas County court-house on Main and Houston Streets.

Although a phalanx of officers were stationed at the court-house, the mob overwhelmed them and made their way to the second-floor courtroom of Judge Robert Sealy, where the prisoner was easily overpowered and one end of a rope was slipped around his neck. The other end was thrown through an open window to the mob waiting two floors below. The victim was pushed and pulled through the open window. Although some said he was killed in the fall, contemporary reports say that Brook's body was dragged by the angry crowd to the corner of Elm and Akard Streets, where he was hanged on a telephone pole—all this to the jeers and cheers of hundreds of Dallasites who watched the action. Although hundreds witnessed the entire event, as was often the case in vigilante actions, no one could be found who could or would identify the perpetrators. One thing is for sure: Despite doubts as to his guilt of the alleged crime, Brooks never got his day in court!

TEXANS LAY CLAIM TO LARGEST TRAIN HEIST
A family of latter-day owlhoots from Callahan County, Texas, who, in the 1920s, replaced galloping horses and bandannas with

automobiles and nitroglycerine, were responsible for the largest train heist in US history. The Newton Boys, who robbed scores of banks from Texas to Canada, seized three million dollars in 1924 from the Chicago, Milwaukee & St. Paul train near Chicago, before they dissolved their gang and resorted to honest work.

In Texas Joe Newton was an excellent bronc rider and his brother Willis, the gang's mastermind, worked for a Uvalde banker and former governor, Dolph Briscoe. Briscoe once described Willis as "a gentleman." The Newton brothers lived to a ripe old age. Jess died in 1960, Doc died in 1974, Willis lived until 1979, and Joe died in 1989.

SANTA CLAUS WOUNDED IN TEXAS GUN BATTLE

"Santa Claus wounded in Texas gun battle" sounds like a tabloid headline, but it's actually true. In an act totally lacking in Yuletide spirit, four bandits, their leader dressed as Santa Claus, entered First National Bank of Cisco on Christmas Eve, 1927, and made off with $12,000. According to newspaper reports, children even followed Santa as he went into the bank. But a shoot-out occurred after police were alerted to the robbery and several people, including Santa, were wounded. The not-so-jolly old elf was captured several days later after a gun battle in South Bend, Texas. Marshall Ratliff ("Santa") was the first of the four robbers to be tried for the crime and was sentenced to die in the electric chair at the state prison in Hunstville. Ratliff was returned to the Eastland County jail on a bench warrant, and in an escape attempt he killed a peace officer, Tom A. "Uncle Tom" Jones, who was helping as a jailer. An angry mob stormed the jail, seized Ratliff, and lynched him.

GEORGE "MACHINE GUN KELLY" BARNES

One of America's most infamous characters of the 1930s put Wise County, Texas, in the headlines in 1933 when, prompted by his ambitious, excitement-craving wife, he kidnapped Oklahoma

millionaire oilman Charles Urschel and held him for ransom on his wife's parents' ranch near the Wise County town of Paradise. George "Machine Gun Kelly" Barnes, a petty bootlegger, had, at the insistence of his wife, gone in to big-time crime and had already robbed a hayseed bank in Wilmer, Texas, taking a small amount of cash and machine-gunning a guard to death. Kelly was buried in the Cottondale Cemetery near Paradise, Texas, when he died of a heart attack in Leavenworth prison in 1954, after being returned there from Alcatraz.

FRANK HAMER, NEMESIS OF THE BARROW GANG

The man who wrote *finis* to the exploits of the infamous team of Clyde Barrow and his youthful moll Bonnie Parker was Texas Ranger captain Francis Augustus Hamer, better known as Frank or Pancho.

Hamer enlisted in the Rangers in 1906. He resigned from the Rangers several times only to return to fight Texas crime. In 1932 Hamer retired from active duty but retained his commission. In 1934 he was recalled by Governor Miriam (Ma) Ferguson to track down the infamous bandit team of Clyde Barrow and Bonnie Parker, who had made themselves a national legend and folk heroes to many who thought them champions of the poor.

After a three-month search, Hamer, with the assistance of other lawmen, trapped the pair, whose name struck terror in the hearts of bankers and lawmen alike, near Gibsland, Louisiana. They were shot and killed in a Hamer-engineered ambush.

LONE STAR WAR STORIES

THE NICKNAME "LONE STAR STATE" COMES DIRECTLY FROM OUR flag, which itself came about as a visual declaration of independence from Mexico. According to the Texas State Library and Archives Commission, in 1839, Stephen F. Austin, William H. Wharton, and Branch T. Archer were sent as commissioners to the federal government to ask for official recognition of Texas as a state. Before taking that step, the trio decided they would be in a better position to seek statehood status if they had an official-looking symbol of Texas's desired status. But that status came at a steep price, which thousands of Texians paid by sacrificing their lives on the battlefield.

However, even that long war was far from being Texas's first rodeo. From the time whites first set foot south of the Red River and west of the Sabine, the Cherokee, Comanche, Kiowa, and other tribes that had called this land home for many generations weren't about to put up with intruders trespassing on their hunting grounds and challenging their livelihood. During the Civil

War and ensuring World Wars, Texans again and again answered the call to fight for their state and nation. Now home to fifteen military bases—and to the first Air Force base—our great state has never forgotten the sacrifices others have made to protect the freedoms we enjoy as citizens of the United States and of the great state of Texas. Here are some of their stories.

SEVENTH FLAG OVER TEXAS

Seven flags over Texas? Anyone familiar with Texas history probably knows that the six flags flown over Texas have represented Spanish rule, French rule, Mexican rule, the independent republic, the Confederacy, and finally the Lone Star State. However, for a short time, there was indeed a seventh flag: that of the "Republican Army of the North." In a plan to free Texas from Spanish rule, José Bernardo Gutiérrez De Lara in 1812 initiated a filibustering expedition in Nachitoches, Louisiana. With the help of US agents, including West Point graduate Augustus William Magee, who was military commander of the Republican Army of the North, a band of rebels and mercenaries crossed the Sabine River into Texas in August and took Nacogdoches.

By November La Bahía at Goliad had fallen to them as well. About 800 filibusters defeated 1,200 royalist troops in the Battle of Rosalis; Governor Manuel de Salcedo surrendered San Antonio on April 1, 1813. Raising the green flag of the Republican Army of the North—sometimes called the "seventh flag over Texas"—Gutierrez and his followers declared the state the "First Republic of Texas."

After Gutierrez permitted the execution of fourteen Spanish officers, however, a disgusted Samuel Kemper, who replaced Magee after his death in February 1813, led more than one hundred troops back to Louisiana. Gutierrez, undaunted, set up a provisional government. Royalist Lieutenant Colonel Ignacio Elizondo besieged San Antonio with about 990 men, and although Gutierrez's troops defeated the Royalists, their growing hostility toward Gutierrez forced him to return to Louisiana. His remaining troops were ambushed and defeated in the Battle of Medina River south of San Antonio.

FIFTY MEXICANS LOSE LIVES IN "GRASS FIGHT"

Two Texians and about fifty Mexican troops lost their lives in what became known as the "Grass Fight." Receiving minimal mention in the annals of Texas history is a bloody skirmish that proved costly to the Mexican troops occupying San Antonio. A rumor reached the Texian army that General Cos had sent Domingo de Ugartechea to Matamoros for reinforcements and silver to be used as pay for his soldiers. Scouts were sent to watch for Ugartechea's return. Erastus "Deaf" Smith spotted a pack train and troops about five miles out of San Antonio. He reported what he assumed were the returning troops and the pack train bearing what was thought to be the silver Cos had requested. On November 26, 1835, Bowie rallied about a hundred men, among whom was Thomas Jefferson Rusk, later to become one of Texas's first senators.

The Texians intercepted the pack train and captured a part of the train, which bore what was assumed to be the silver. In the ensuing fight, two Texians and about fifty Mexicans lost their lives. Instead of reinforcements, however, the soldiers turned out to be a foraging party sent out to find and gather grass for the Mexican army's horses. The "bags of silver" turned out to be bags of grass to be used as fodder for the horses. The bloody battle was a costly one and all for naught!

THE "COME AND TAKE IT" FLAG

The story of the "come and take it" flag is one that is often overlooked. The town of Gonzales was the westernmost point of Anglo American civilization in Texas in 1836. Much of the Texas revolutionary activity was centered there, such as the Battle of Gonzales on October 2, 1835. The town was known as "The Lexington of the Texas Revolution," as the first battle of the revolution was fought there. The battle grew out of Mexican demands for a cannon that had been given to the colonists at Gonzales for defense against the Indians. The Mexicans sent troops to take the cannon, but it had been buried in a peach orchard for preservation. When a Mexican officer and his troops arrived, they dug up the cannon, mounted it on oxcart wheels, loaded it with pieces of chain and scrap iron, and used it to fire the first shot of the Texans' war for independence from Mexico. To taunt the Mexicans the Texans hung up a flag that reputedly bore a rough picture of the cannon and the words, "Come and take it!"

REMEMBER THE ALAMO

Legend has it that in the Battle of San Jacinto, in which Texas won her independence from Mexico, many Mexican soldiers were heard making the plaintive cry, "Me no Alamo! Me no Goliad!" The suppliants made these pleas in hopes of receiving mercy from the Texans by disavowing involvement in the two best-known massacres of Texans. At the Alamo many Texans died because of Santa Anna's orders to "show no mercy." And on March 27, 1836, Colonel James Fannin and 352 of his soldiers were executed though they were prisoners of war held at Presidio La Bahía at Goliad. Subsequently the Texans' battle cry became "Remember the Alamo; remember Goliad!" Keenly aware of the atrocities they had committed, the Mexicans knew the wrath of the Texans and sought every way possible not to become victims of it.

SANTA ANNA SHOWS MERCY

Santa Anna's brutality at the Alamo is well known, but historians tell us of at least one act of benevolence on his part after the battle of the Alamo, when the Mexican general ordered his soldiers to collect the bodies of the defenders to be burned. One of the soldiers, Francisco Esparza, began searching for the body of his brother, Gregorio, who had fought with the defenders. When he found the body, he and his widowed sister-in-law went to

Santa Anna and begged permission to give Gregorio a Christian burial. Santa Anna granted permission, and Gregorio Esparza was removed and buried near the San Fernando church, the only Alamo defender accorded such an honor.

TEJANO HEROES

Texans of Mexican heritage are generally known as Mexican Americans; early Texans of Mexican descent were called Tejanos. Many Tejanos played important roles in settling Texas and helping her to gain independence from Mexico. A few of our Tejano heroes were Juan Seguin, Gregorio Esparza (mentioned above), and Lorenzo De Zavala. It should be noted that Esparza fought in the Alamo on the side of Texas, while his brother fought with Santa Anna's army.

BRIEF BUT MONUMENTAL BATTLE

The Battle of San Jacinto, fought on April 21, 1836, was a pivotal one for Texas as it led to nationhood, then statehood, but this weighty event actually took place in a brief amount of time: eighteen minutes. The Texans lost only nine men, and thirty-four were wounded.

NAPOLEON OF THE WEST CAUGHT

Although little has been written about the capture of the "Napoleon of the West," as Santa Anna liked to call himself, his positive identification at the time he was captured can be credited to his own troops. According to the *Handbook of Texas*, "Santa Anna, who had disappeared during the battle, was discovered by James A. Sylvester and others on April 22 and was recognized by the Mexican prisoners when he was brought into camp." The Texans were not sure they had captured Santa Anna at first because of his less-than-grandiose dress. His identity was revealed by the Mexican prisoners, whose homage gave him away.

MASONIC "DISTRESS SIGNAL" SPARED SANTA ANNA

You never know when that "secret handshake" might save your bacon: Santa Anna's life was spared after he was captured and identified at San Jacinto, and he was brought before Sam Houston, whose men wanted to execute him immediately. Texas historians have written that since Santa Anna and Houston were both Masons, Santa Anna gave the Masonic "distress signal" and Houston intervened to spare his life.

THE "RUNAWAY SCRAPE"

The term "runaway scrape" is the term Texians applied to the flight from their homes when Mexican general Santa Anna began his effort to conquer Texas in February of 1836. The first persons involved in the flight were those residing in the south central portion of Texas, such as San Patricio, Refugio, and San Antonio. The Texians started to leave when news came that the Mexicans were gathering on the Rio Grande.

After Sam Houston learned of the fate of the Alamo, he decided to retreat and ordered all inhabitants to accompany him. People began to flee, leaving everything to make a flight to safety. Houston's retreat to regroup and find a suitable place to fight Santa Anna marked the beginning of the "Runaway Scrape."

With Houston's army gone, the settlers were left without protection from the Mexicans; the remaining settlers fled, making their way toward Louisiana or Galveston Island. Although David G. Burnet ordered Houston to halt and make a stand, Houston continued to retreat. The settlers' flight was marked by a lack of preparation and panic caused by fear of both the Mexican army and the Indians. The fleeing settlers used any means of transportation or none at all. Many people died and were buried where they fell. In the meantime, Sam Houston had taken up a position with the Texian army at San Jacinto. It was there that the general made his stand against the self-proclaimed "Napoleon of the West."

The settlers' flight continued until they learned of Houston's decisive victory at San Jacinto. Because so many false rumors persisted as to the military status of the Texian army, Houston's victory was received with skepticism. But gradually the settlers began to retrace their steps and return home. Many found their homes existed no more. The gallant thirteen-day stand of the Alamo defenders had given Houston the necessary time to regroup, decide on a place to challenge the Mexicans, and develop a strategy that resulted in his victory and independence for Texas.

Black Bean Death Warrant

The "Black Bean Death Warrant" is one of Texas's most interesting bits of trivia, although not trivial to those involved. In December of 1842 a party of Texan soldiers on what was known as the Mier Expedition crossed the border seeking supplies from Mexico. Mexicans captured 176 of the soldiers and all were sentenced to be shot. Then the order was changed and it was decided instead that every tenth man would be shot. An earthen pot containing 159 white beans and 17 black beans was presented to the captured

soldiers and each was instructed to draw a bean. Those who drew the black beans were to be shot; the black beans were their "death warrant." One man noticed that the black beans seemed to be larger than the white ones and fingered the beans until he found a smaller one and drew it out. It was indeed a white bean, and the lucky soldier survived.

Although much has been written about the Black Bean incident, what happened to the remains of the seventeen shot as a result of drawing the black bean is almost lost in the footnotes of history. The bodies of the men were brought back from Mexico and buried at what is now known as Monument Hill, near LaGrange, Texas.

THREE PRESIDENTS-TO-BE IN BATTLE

The battle of Palo Alto, the first battle of the Mexican War, had two unique features. On May 8, 1846, twelve miles northeast of Brownsville, US General Zachary Taylor's 2,228 men defeated a Mexican force of twice as many men. The battle was the first time in the Americas that the United States had used lightweight mobile artillery. Another unique feature was that the battle brought together three future presidents. Taylor became US president in 1848. In his command was a young lieutenant, Ulysses S. Grant, who became eighteenth president of the United States. The defeated Mexicans were under command of Mariano Arista, who became president of Mexico in 1851.

BUFFALO SOLDIERS:
FROM CANNON FODDER TO TEXAS HEROES

It was not until the horrific carnage of the Civil War that black Americans were permitted to serve in the regular US Army. When it became evident that the fierce fighting was going to decimate the Union fighting forces, which were made up of white Americans, those in command decided that black slaves would be accepted on a volunteer basis to serve in the US Army. This, they reasoned, would save the lives of thousands of white American soldiers destined to be claimed by the ferocious fighting. The first black men accepted to fight alongside white soldiers were accepted literally as cannon fodder. Many white officers refused to command black troops, feeling them unequal to the task of soldiering. Before long the bravery shown by the black soldiers who died by the thousands as Confederate forces mowed them down at the front lines was enough to mellow the opinions of white officers. Before the conflict was over, praise was being heaped on the blacks by all but the die-hard racist white officers. These first black soldiers performed in such a way that their ability could no longer be doubted.

The Civil War laid the groundwork for some of Texas's most heroic and often unheralded heroes, those black troopers known as the "Buffalo Soldiers." During the Indian Wars between 1866 and 1891, the time of Texas's settlement toward its westward border, ten thousand black men made up 20 percent of the cavalry and 10 percent of the entire US Army. They were nicknamed Buffalo Soldiers by the Indians because their wooly hair resembled that of the buffalo. Having overcome the prejudices of their white counterparts, they were assigned to forts that had been established along the Texas western frontier to protect the mail route between San Antonio and El Paso and to protect travelers and settlers attempting to expand Texas's civilization westward.

Following the Civil War the United States formed two Cavalry Regiments, the Ninth and Tenth Cavalry. These units were made up of black soldiers who wanted to remain in the army after the Civil War. Their mission was to control hostile Indians who stood in the way of settlers invading the Great Plains.

Named for Jefferson Davis, secretary of war and later president of the Confederacy, Fort Davis in Jeff Davis County was established in 1854. It was abandoned by the army during the Civil War. Buffalo Soldiers were sent to reoccupy it in 1867. The fighting prowess of the Buffalo Soldiers won the respect of whites and Indians alike.

"Treue der Union" Monument

It is doubtful that one can find a more deserved monument to patriotism in Texas than the one that stands in the Hill Country town of Comfort. This Kendall County town was settled by Germans from the town of New Braunfels in 1854. Wearied by their journey, they were charmed by the scenery and sparkling water. They called the place "Camp Comfort."

The outbreak of the Civil War divided Texans into two camps, Secessionists and Union sympathizers (those, like Sam Houston, who wanted to avoid splitting the Union). A band of residents of Comfort, mostly Germans, who were Unionists left Comfort en route to Mexico. On August 10, 1862, the sixty-five men encamped on the Nueces River were attacked by ninety-four mounted Confederate soldiers. Nineteen Unionists were killed and nine were wounded. The wounded were executed later. Of the thirty-seven who escaped the battle, six were killed while trying to cross into Mexico. Eleven reached home, and most of the remaining twenty escaped temporarily to Mexico or California. The monument "Treue der Union" (True to the Union) commemorates the battle of the Nueces and bears the names of the victims of the battle.

"The Great Hanging"

The largest mass hanging by a "duly constituted court" involved the hanging of thirty-nine residents of the Confederate State of Texas in Gainesville in October 1862. "The great hanging" grew out of an alleged "Peace Party conspiracy," which prompted Confederate authorities to suppress it. The military authorities penetrated a secret organization said to number several hundred men.

On October 1, 1862, armed forces carried out raids in Cooke County and took sixty to seventy men into custody, bringing them to Gainesville and placing them under guard. On the same day, Colonel William C. Young, commander of the Texas Cavalry, presided over a meeting. He created a "citizens' court" that was instructed to examine all crimes and offenses committed, determine the guilt or innocence of the accused, and pronounce appropriate punishment. The court, in the succeeding weeks, found guilty thirty-nine of those charged and sentenced them to be hanged. The sentences were carried out in Gainesville.

GRAVE OF THE CONFEDERACY

It is doubtful that many of us know where in Texas the "grave of the Confederacy" is located. The story behind this thought-provoking item is as follows: In May of 1865, just after the collapse of the Confederacy, General Joseph Orville Shelby, commander of the Missouri Raiders, who were stationed in Texas at the time of Robert E. Lee's surrender, led his brigade across Texas and into Mexico. This was known as the Shelby Expedition. Shelby refused to surrender. His troops were estimated variously at between three thousand and twelve thousand. When some one thousand reached Piedras Negras, which is across from Eagle Pass, they buried their Confederate flag at the Rio Grande in a ceremony that became known as "the grave of the Confederacy incident."

LAST SURVIVING CIVIL WAR SOLDIER

When honorary general Walter Williams died in 1959 at the age of 117, one of America's most important periods of history came to an end. Williams was the last surviving soldier of the Civil War, having served in Hood's Texas Brigade during the final months of the war. When the last surviving Union soldier died in 1956, Dwight Eisenhower bestowed upon Williams the honorary rank of general. He was buried in a Confederate general's uniform.

WON BY A VERY LONG SHOT

The last hostile Indian attack on whites in Texas occurred in 1874 at Adobe Walls in Hutchinson County. The raid was instigated by a war-mongering medicine man and led by Comanche Chief

Quanah Parker, who assembled a war party and attacked the buffalo hunters' camp. Chief Parker, the last Comanche Indian chief, was the son of an Indian father and a white mother, Cynthia Ann Parker, who was captured as a small girl at Fort Parker, Texas. Some contend that the last hostile action with Indians in Texas was after 1874 when General Ranald S. Mackenzie defeated a large force of Indians at Palo Duro Canyon, one of the last Indian strongholds in the state, in order for Anglo Americans to make a permanent settlement in the area. However, few will dispute what ended the Adobe Walls attack: One eagle-eye buffalo hunter shot a Comanche off his horse from nearly a mile away.

CONGRESSIONAL MEDAL OF HONOR

The only battle in history in which every military participant received the Congressional Medal of Honor took place in Texas in 1874. In the "Buffalo Wallow fight" in the Panhandle county of Hemphill near the Washita River, William (Billy) Dixon, who was carrying dispatches to Fort Supply, was surrounded by a band of Comanche and Kiowa warriors. With five companions, Dixon decided to make a stand. Four of the men were wounded before noon. Dixon located a buffalo wallow about ten feet wide some distance away and ran for it, suffering a flesh wound in the leg on the way. Dixon shouted for his comrades to come and then ran back to carry a man who had a broken leg. All day the Indians circled the men, making occasional forays.

At nightfall the Indians stopped. One man was sent to find help but failed to find the trail. Dixon found the trail and discovered a body of mounted men in the distance that turned out to be US troops. Their commander refused them ammunition and left them, promising to notify the commander of a camp in Gray County of their condition. One man was buried at Buffalo Wallow and the five survivors were taken to Fort Supply. The five survivors received the Medal of Honor on General Miles's recommendation.

After an illustrious career, Dixon became postmaster when a post office was established at Adobe Walls in 1884. He married Olive King, who for three years thereafter was the only woman in Hutchinson County! Dixon died in 1913. Since the Indian wars of the nineteenth century, sixty-five Texans have earned the highest honor for valor bestowed by an appreciative nation—the Congressional Medal of Honor. Thirty-seven of these have been awarded posthumously after recipients sacrificed their own lives for their comrades and their nation.

Army Air Corps Born in Texas

The US Army Air Corps was actually born in Texas. Military aviation began in San Antonio in February 1910 when Lieutenant Benjamin Foulois arrived at Fort Sam Houston with seventeen crates containing an airplane, accompanied by a number of student mechanics. Foulois, assigned to the aviation section of the US Army Signal Corps, had taken three flying lessons from Wilbur Wright. Because of the winter weather at the Signal Corps facility at College Park, Maryland, flight training was moved to Fort Sam Houston. Foulois had orders to assemble the plane, learn to fly it, and train others to fly it.

The aircraft was a Wright Brothers biplane with a wingspan of 36 feet, 4 inches, and an overall length of 32 feet, 10 inches. The power plant was a four-cylinder, water-cooled 30.6-horsepower Wright engine. Instead of wheels, the plane was equipped with sleigh-like runners. Takeoff was aided by a sort of catapult. The plane was ready to fly by March 1. By the outbreak of World War I in 1917, the US Army Signal Corps had thirty-five trained pilots and two hundred training planes. Foulois proved that aviation could be a vital part of military operations and helped establish Texas as a major military aviation center. He rose to the rank of major general and became chief of the Air Corps before he retired in 1935.

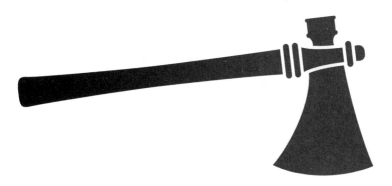

The "Lost Battalion"

A number of unwilling Texans allegedly participated in the building of the bridge made famous in the post-WWII book, movie, and song *The Bridge on the River Kwai*. These reluctant Texas workers were members of the 2nd Battalion, 131st Field Artillery of the 36th Infantry Division of the Texas National Guard. Later dubbed "The Lost Battalion" by newspapers, this battalion, along with Dutch, Australian, and British forces, surrendered to invading Japanese forces on Java. They were taken prisoners of war, and the United States could not or would not disclose what happened to the unit, thus the nickname, "The Lost Battalion." Over the next forty-two months, the men were confined to such projects as building roads and railroad construction, including building the now-famous bridge over the River Kwai.

Buildings Literally in Ship Shape

Two Texas heroes are associated with buildings in the shape of steamboats. The home of Sam Houston in Hunstville was called Steamboat House because it was constructed in the shape of a riverboat. The Admiral Nimitz Museum in Fredericksburg, honoring World War II fleet hero Chester Nimitz, is housed in his grandfather's old Steamboat Hotel. It, too, was built in the shape of a riverboat.

THERE OUGHT TO BE A LAW . . .

LAWS ARE IN PLACE FOR A GOOD NUMBER OF REASONS, THE BEST of which are to protect lives and property, but the rationales behind some laws can be downright befuddling. The whys and wherefores that explain how some people come to be voted into office can be just as mystifying. But people have their reasons, and sometimes they take the time to write them down to make sure future generations at least know *how* some things happened, if not exactly *why*. If you've ever wondered, "How did that law ever get passed?" or "How did he or she ever get elected?" you may find the answer in this chapter—but I'm not making any promises.

A LEAGUE AND A LABOR

To many who have studied Texas history, the term "a league and a labor" has managed to slip from our recollection. We were taught that this term was a Spanish land measurement and was the amount of land granted to the heads of the households of the first Anglo settlers. A labor was a Spanish land unit measuring 177 acres. Under the Mexican Colonization Act by which the first settlers entered the Stephen F. Austin colony in Texas, heads of families engaged in farming received a labor of land. Cattle raisers received a *sitio* or league (4,428 acres). Most settlers combined ranching and farming and got a league and a labor.

Married with Children

The bonds of matrimony, though an institution now, were more of a convenience to the early settlers of Texas. Priests were not widely available, and a couple might live together as man and wife for quite a while before a priest came along to make the union legal. Mass weddings, in which area couples gathered for one community ceremony when the priest came to town, were common practice, as was something called *bond matrimony*. This involved the couple going before the alcalde (mayor) and making a bond, written very much like the wedding vows used today. This was acceptable until a priest became available. Sometimes a long time passed before a priest came to a colony, and many couples already had children!

Texans Support Santa Anna

At one time, believe it or not, Texans were on the side of Santa Anna. In October of 1832 delegates from sixteen Texas districts met at San Felipe and voted their support for a revolutionary trying to overthrow the Mexican government. His name: Antonio López de Santa Anna.

The Knights of Texas

There was a time when knighthood was bestowed upon certain Texans. Sam Houston created the Order of San Jacinto between 1842 and January 1843 during his second term as president of the Republic of Texas. In 1939 the Sons of the Republic of Texas revived the Order of San Jacinto so that they could honor distinguished Texans.

Rushed Annexation of Texas

One foreign power was against the annexation of Texas into the United States. Great Britain opposed it and even contemplated force to prevent it! Britain did not want to add Texas to the British

Empire, but they wanted to prevent the westward expansion of the United States to reap the commercial advantages of Texas trade. Britain's policy toward Texas so alarmed Americans that the annexation was pushed through quickly and was completed on December 29, 1845.

FIFTY CENT ACT
The Fifty Cent Act advocated by Governor O. M. Roberts was approved by the Texas legislature on July 14, 1879. It provided for selling Texas public land at fifty cents an acre, one half of the proceeds to be used for paying the public debt and the other half to be used to establish a public school fund. The act opened to settlement about fifty-two West Texas counties, out of which 3,201,283 acres were sold for $1,600,645.55. The act was repealed in January 1883.

CAR-BARN CONVENTION
Although it might seem like an unconventional place for a political convention, one Texas governor was nominated for office in a streetcar barn! The Democratic state convention of August 1892 met in the Houston streetcar barn because it was the only building large enough to accommodate all the delegates. The "car-barn convention" nominated James Hogg, who was reelected governor that same year.

THE FIVE STATES OF TEXAS?
Biographers say Texas politician and former vice president of the United States John Nance "Cactus Jack" Garner of Uvalde, Texas, introduced a bill in the 1899 session of the Texas legislature that, if passed, would have divided Texas into five states. His stated reasoning was to "increase Lone Star representation in the United States Congress." Although the idea of dividing Texas sounds preposterous if not downright treasonous to the average Texan, Garner's idea was not without foundation. According to

the book *Annexation of Texas,* published in 1919, "The resolution of Congress allowing the annexation of Texas had the provision that Texas could be divided into states of a convenient size not to exceed four in addition to the said state of Texas." This verbiage allows for five states. Garner's proposal did not pass.

MISSOURI CAPITAL IN TEXAS

Marshall, Texas, was at one time the capital of Missouri. How, you ask? Well, after the fall of Vicksburg to Union forces in 1863, the city of Marshall became the civil authority west of the Mississippi River, and as a fortified city, it housed the capital of the state of Missouri. It remained the capital until the South capitulated. Governor Thomas C. Reynolds and his staff had their headquarters there.

CAPITOL COUP

Voter fraud is nothing new in the world of politics, and anyone would be hard-pressed to find a state in the United States whose history hasn't been tarnished by it. But how many states can say a military coup has taken place in their capitol? The gubernatorial election of 1873, in which Richard Coke defeated E. J. Davis 85,549 votes to 42,663, had been characterized by fraud and intimidation on both sides. The Supreme Court held that the election was illegal, and Davis, the Republican incumbent, maintained that he had a right to finish out his four-year term. Nevertheless, the Democrats secured keys to the second floor of the capitol and took possession. Davis reportedly had troops stationed on the lower floor.

The Texas Rifles, summoned to protect Davis, were converted into a sheriff's posse and protected Coke. The tense situation went on from January 16 to 17, 1874, until a telegram from President Ulysses S. Grant indicated that he did not feel warranted to send out federal troops to keep Davis in office. Coke's inauguration restored Democratic control in Texas.

Semicolon Court

The "Semicolon Court" is a historic and derisive appellation given to the Supreme Court of Texas during Reconstruction in Texas. The name was given because the court invalidated the general election of 1873 based on the placement of a semicolon in Section 6, Article 3 of the Constitution of 1869.

The Capitol Syndicate

One organization that has fallen through the cracks of Texas history is the Capitol Syndicate. Without it, we wouldn't have been able to boast that our great state had the largest fenced-in ranch in the world during the late nineteenth century.

In 1879, the Sixteenth Legislature appropriated three million acres of land to finance a new capitol building. After the state capitol burned down in 1881, the construction of a new building understandably became a top priority. Mattheas Schnell of Rock Island, Illinois, was awarded the contract in return for the acreage. Schnell then formed the "Capitol Syndicate" to get investors to provide the funds to build the capitol. Since the land the investors were to receive as payment was in the unsettled Texas Panhandle, the syndicate established the XIT Ranch to utilize the land until it could be sold.

Bonham's "Mr. Speaker," Sam Rayburn

Sam Rayburn was Speaker of the House of Representatives longer than any other man. This man who was the epitome of a politician was born in 1882, the son of a Confederate soldier who refused to accept a commission because of his embarrassment over his inability to read or write. Rayburn moved to Texas when he was five years old. He attended country schools and developed an interest in politics. On the brink of a new century, Texas's first native-born governor, Jim Hogg, was in office.

Rayburn attended Mayo Normal School, now East Texas University in Commerce. He worked at three jobs to support himself. He passed a teachers' examination and taught in Hopkins County for a year before returning to Commerce to finish getting a degree, which was conferred upon him in 1903. Rayburn, the son of an illiterate soldier, won a seat in the House in 1907. He admittedly was afraid of town folks in store-bought clothes.

Prior to election to the legislature, Sam Rayburn had never been a hundred miles from home. In 1911, at age twenty-nine, Rayburn became the youngest Speaker of the Texas House. When the congressman from Bonham decided to run for the US Senate, Rayburn announced for Congress. He was elected after a difficult campaign. One of his mentors in Congress was Congressman—later vice president under Franklin Roosevelt—John Nance Garner of Uvalde, Texas.

Following the death of Speaker William Bankhead in 1940, Rayburn became the ninety-second Speaker. It was Rayburn who in 1945, when he became aware that Roosevelt was near death, told friends, "I'll have to speak with Harry [Truman] tomorrow. He has to be prepared to carry on a tremendous burden." Truman was in Rayburn's office on April 12, when White House aides located him to inform him of the president's death.

On January 31, 1951, Rayburn exceeded three thousand days as Speaker of the House. Rayburn was once quoted as saying, in regard to his ascension to power, "I missed being a tenant farmer by a gnat's heel."

John Nance "Cactus Jack" Garner

One example of our state's political luminaries was the thirty-second vice president of the United States, John Nance "Cactus Jack" Garner.

Garner grew up in a Red River County, Texas, log cabin as the oldest of thirteen children. He earned pocket money playing shortstop for the semipro Coon Soup Hollow Blossom Prairie baseball team. As a lifetime devotee of baseball, Garner was a familiar figure at baseball games in Washington, D.C.

This colorful Texas epitome of a politician didn't start at the top of the political ladder. After spending a semester at Vanderbilt, Garner developed tuberculosis and returned to a drier Texas climate, where he read law with a law firm. In his first venture into politics, he was defeated in his bid for the office of city attorney. It was shortly thereafter that he moved to the South Texas town of Uvalde. While a partner in a law firm, he was appointed to fill a vacancy as county judge. He later won an elected term in his office. Garner was elected to the state legislature in 1898. It was as a state legislator that he gained his lifelong nickname, "Cactus Jack." His love for the prickly pear caused him to introduce the bloom of this prolific cactus as the state flower of Texas. The Colonial Dames of Texas spoke for the bluebonnet, including presenting an oil painting of that flower to the legislators, many of whom had never seen one, and got the bluebonnet designated as the state flower. "Cactus Jack" lost his bid for the cactus.

It was also as a state legislator that he launched his long-lasting national political career. He won approval of a plan to redistrict a part of South Texas. Not unexpectedly, he ran for and was elected to represent the newly created district in the US Congress.

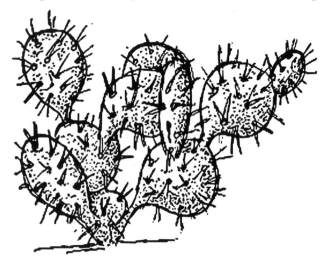

Garner was thirty-five years old when he went to Washington as Democratic Representative of the Fifteenth Texas Congressional District. Theodore Roosevelt was president.

By the time World War I came upon us, Garner was recognized as the leading Democrat. Although he was considered an isolationist, he voted to declare war on Germany. In Garner's twenty-eighth year in politics, he was elected to the high position of Speaker of the US House of Representatives. He was also mentioned as a possible candidate for the presidency. History tells us that Franklin Roosevelt won the nomination with Garner selected as his vice presidential running mate. Roosevelt's success in politics is legendary, and although Garner disapproved of Roosevelt's seeking a third term, he remained a staunch Democrat.

He returned to Uvalde after thirty-eight years in the nation's capital. This bright Texas star was the first Texan to be elected to Speaker of the House and the first Texan elected vice president. "Cactus Jack" Garner remained a political voice and lived to endorse John F. Kennedy in 1960 and fellow Texan Lyndon Baines Johnson in 1964. The "Sage of Uvalde" died in 1967 just days shy of his ninety-ninth birthday.

JIM FERGUSON

One of the most written-about political faux pas was made by former governor Jim Ferguson, who served from 1915 to 1917. After being embroiled in a scandal that resulted in his impeachment—on the heels of a grand jury indictment by Travis County for seven counts of misapplication of public funds, one count of embezzlement, and one count of diversion of public funds—"Farmer Jim" included the following statement in his reelection campaign speech: "Two years ago you elected the best governor money could buy. Now elect the best governor patriotism can give you." A frank critic might say this was Farmer Jim's most truthful speech. Although he won reelection, he was found guilty as charged and thrown out of office shortly after beginning his second term.

Miriam A. "Ma" Ferguson

Thousands of people from all over Texas traveled to Austin in January 1925 to see Miriam Ferguson take the oath of office as Texas's first woman governor. Records indicate that many women were present to see one of their own assume the highest executive office in the state, marking another milestone in their fight for equal rights. Ferguson, who was married to former governor Jim (also known as "Pa") Ferguson, decided to run for office when the Democratic party refused to nominate her husband, who challenged his impeachment. She served two nonconsecutive terms.

W. Lee "Pappy" O'Daniel

A political unknown in Fort Worth campaigned against the very law that kept him from voting—and won! In 1938, W. Lee (Pappy) O'Daniel, general manager of a Fort Worth flour mill and promoter of a popular western swing radio band, entered the Democratic race for governor of Texas against twelve opponents, four of them seasoned politicians (including Miriam Ferguson). O'Daniel was unknown in politics and unable to even vote because he hadn't paid his poll tax. Making use of another group of "hill-billy" musicians in his campaign, his platform focused on "The Golden Rule," the promise of a state pension for Texas elderly, and the elimination of the poll tax. O'Daniel won with an incredible 51 percent of the votes. Despite little success following through with his campaign promises, he was reelected in 1940. Then, in a special election in 1941, he ran for and was elected to represent Texas as a senator in the US Congress—narrowly winning the Democratic nomination against then-Representative Lyndon B. Johnson.

Landslide Lyndon

The city of Alice in Jim Wells County and neighboring Duval County are unalterably linked to the political scandal that is still examined fifty years later. The year is 1948, and Texan Lyndon B. Johnson is locked in political combat with popular Coke Stevenson for a US Senate seat. Stevenson had apparently won the bitterly fought race until an amended tally from precinct 13 in Jim Wells County gave Johnson enough additional votes to win the election by a margin of *eighty-seven* votes out of a million votes cast. This squeaker gave Johnson a nickname that would stay with him until he died: "Landslide Lyndon." Johnson was accused of stealing the election with the help of political boss George Parr, known as "The Duke of Duval," who allegedly had the ballot box stuffed in Johnson's favor. This was a giant step in the direction of the White House.

Monumental Name Ban

Some historians have written that a dispute over the size of the letters to be inscribed on the cornerstone of one of Texas's best-loved monuments threatened its construction. When the San Jacinto Monument was being built at the site of the battlefield near Houston, a flap arose when the Daughters of the Republic of Texas learned that the names of Franklin D. Roosevelt, Gov. James Allred, and Jesse Jones were to be inscribed in 1¼-inch letters, while the names of the 1836 heroes were relegated to letters of ¼-inch on the stone. A call to arms and a few meetings of the DRT at the state capitol at Austin resulted in legislation that banned the names of any living person on state monuments. On San Jacinto Day, April 21, 1937, Jesse Jones laid the cornerstone. No names were carved into the Cordova shell stone.

Will Travel for Sugar

There was a time when Mexico meant the difference in Texans having or not having that special cake or pie! We depended on our neighbors to the south for the sugar that enabled us to make that Sunday treat. In the 1940s, when World War II brought about the rationing of sugar, Texans along the Rio Grande River trekked across the bridges into Mexico to bring back supplies of the coveted sweetener.

CHRYSLER'S DODGE TEXAN

In 1956 the Chrysler Corporation produced an automobile model specially to be sold in Texas. Called the Dodge Texan, its sales brochures boasted, "The name is proudly emblazoned on both rear fenders. And the brave crossed flags of the Lone Star State are right up front where your fellow Texans can admire them." The crossed flags were indeed prominently displayed on the front of the automobile. This was, unfortunately, in violation of the protocol for use of the Texas flag, which says, "Pictures of the flag shall not be used in an advertisement." According to Chrysler representatives, the emblems were used for three months until a complaint was filed by the Daughters of the Republic of Texas. Subsequently the flags were removed.

THE WET TOWN THAT DRIED UP

Texas has at least one town that was incorporated solely for the purpose of selling liquor. The State of Texas allows some areas to elect whether to prohibit the sale of alcohol, and these areas are known as "wet" or "dry" depending on which they choose through popular vote. In 1960 the town of Impact was incorporated just outside of Abilene in Taylor County. Named for Mayor Dallas Perkins's advertising business, the town covered forty-seven square miles and was best known for being the only wet town in dry Taylor County. When two liquor stores opened, a couple of Abilene lawyers went to court to oppose the town's incorporation. In 1963 the Texas Supreme Court upheld the incorporation and the sale of liquor. The town flourished for sixteen years, building streets and making improvements, but eventually "dried up" after Abilene was voted wet in 1976 and Impact was no longer the closest place to buy alcoholic beverages.

ONLY IN TEXAS

EVERY STATE HAS ITS TRADITIONS, ICONS, AND SAYINGS THAT are unique to its history and culture. If you've ever wondered why a state whose official flower is the bluebonnet would have a state song about a yellow rose or what day Juneteenth falls on and what it signifies or why you can't just relax in your seat during a Texas A&M game, read on . . .

GONE TO TEXAS

Many settlers saw Texas as a land of "greener pastures," a real opportunity. Some of them were in such a hurry to get here that they took little time to notify family and friends as to where they had gone. Some simply put up signs that said, "GTT," which meant "Gone to Texas." The land, however, attracted its share of those outside the law. The expression "GTT" came into use when Texas developed the reputation of harboring outlaws who had fled to Texas to seek refuge. Some historians have written that GTT was appended to the names of lawbreakers who skipped out and, in some cases, to new arrivals to Texas who were suspected of leaving home under suspicious circumstances.

THE YELLOW ROSE OF TEXAS

The popular state ballad "The Yellow Rose of Texas" isn't just about a flower—it is a tribute to a lovely young girl who did much in her own way to help the Texans win their independence from Mexico. Historical accounts say that the "yellow rose" was Emily Morgan, a young mulatto slave girl whom Santa Anna had captured at the James Morgan household and put to work for himself.

Emily had been loyal to the Texans and had been able to pass information to them at San Jacinto. It is said that, about the time the Battle of San Jacinto started, she had General Santa Anna "occupied" in his tent. This gave the Texans a definite battle advantage and allowed them to capture Santa Anna literally with his pants down! According to Martha Anne Turner's book *The Yellow Rose of Texas: Her Saga and Her Song,* Texans were already in Santa Anna's camp killing Mexican soldiers when he appeared in his red slippers and underwear. The song refers to Emily's skin color.

SIESTA THEORY

Some events in Texas history have been edited or "censored" when teaching them to schoolchildren because they were deemed inappropriate for young ears. One such event is the story of how Santa Anna lost the battle at San Jacinto. The "siesta theory," which many Texas youngsters were taught in school, is that the Mexican leader was caught napping when the Texans attacked!

HAZARDOUS OCCUPATION

The job of surveyor today doesn't seem like such a dangerous occupation. But in the early days of Texas, settlers often hired surveyors to locate their land and stake it out, payment being one-third of the total acreage. The risk for this reward was great: Indians recognized surveying equipment as "the thing that stole the land," and when the men with the instruments showed up to take away their hunting land, they attacked whenever possible.

JUNETEENTH

One of Texas's most important anniversaries is known by a nickname. June 19 is the date in 1865 when Union General Granger announced, for the first time, the emancipation of Texas slaves. Texas blacks celebrate this day as "Juneteenth."

"The Eyes of Texas" Prank

"The Eyes of Texas," the official song of the University of Texas and accepted by most as the unofficial state song of Texas, was originally written as a prank! According to the *Handbook of Texas*, the Glee Club at UT serenaded school president William L. Prather at a varsity minstrel show in 1903 with lyrics written by John Lang Sinclair sung to the tune of "I've Been Working on the Levee." The words were a take-off of the president's frequent admonition to students, "The eyes of Texas are upon you!" The song became popular with the entire student body and was adopted as the official song of UT. It took on a more serious tone when students were asked to sing it at Prather's funeral in 1905.

Texas A&M's Twelfth Man

You probably don't need to watch the movie (or TV series) *Friday Night Lights* to know that football not only is a vital part of Texas culture but has generated its share of unique and noteworthy stories. Take the poignant tale of Texas A&M University's legendary "twelfth man."

"Non-Aggies" attending an A&M game for the first time are amazed to see the entire student body stand throughout the entire game, except during half-time, at which time they may sit. This strange tradition is based on an event that took place in January 1922 during the "Dixie Classic," the forerunner of the Cotton Bowl.

The game was played at Fair Park in Dallas and pitted A&M against Centre College in a bitter contest. According to Kern Tips's *Football Texas Style*, the A&M squad was suffering; injuries had depleted the team to the point that coach Dana Bible wasn't sure he would have enough players to finish the game. Then the coach remembered seeing former player E. King Gill (whom he had released from football to play basketball) sitting in the stands.

Coach Bible had Gill brought down from the stands and suited up on the sidelines so that he would be available to play if needed; Gill thus became the team's twelfth man. Though the team went on to enjoy a sweet victory that date, it wasn't nearly as precious as the tradition that had been started for the Aggies. Since that unusual "recruitment," A&M fans stand ready, as a body, to show their willingness to play if needed, to be the twelfth man.

TEXAS-LEAGUER

One little bit of Texas that has influenced another popular national pastime is the term "Texas-leaguer," which can be heard on televised baseball games. A Texas-leaguer is a fly ball that is hit too far to be snagged by an infielder but too short to be caught by an outfielder. How this term came to be associated with Texas is not known, but ball player Harry Raymond is said to have coined the term in 1888.

A PRICKLY TOPIC

A sticky subject to touch on is the Texas cactus. Some one hundred species of the prickly plant are found in Texas, the widest assortment found in any single state in the United States. They range from the common prickly pear cactus (which is the official state plant) to a rare variety found only in El Paso. Texas also grows cacti of radically different sizes, from the button cactus, which is no larger than a dime, to the barrel cactus, also known as the fishhook cactus, which can weigh in at half a ton. As formidable as their protective spines may seem, however, with proper preparation many cacti can be eaten by humans and livestock.

Texas cacti have an interesting array of names as well, from pleasant to amusing to downright painful-sounding. These include hunger, starvation, flapjack, dumpling, strawberry, blind pear, cow's tongue, night blooming, devil's head, horse-killer, rainbow, pin cushion, porcupine, lady-finger, and "Glory of Texas" (which, oddly enough, grows mainly in Mexico!).

STATE FISH
The Guadalupe bass, a member of the sunfish family, was named the official state fish of Texas by the Seventy-First Legislature in 1989. This particular fish was chosen because it's found only in the freshwater streams and rivers of Texas.

INFLATED CURRENCY
During the period of the Republic of Texas, notes signed by individuals promising to pay a cow and a calf passed as a ten-dollar bill, even though a cow and a calf were not worth ten American dollars!

REDBACKS
While most people are familiar with the term "greenbacks," there was a time when the Republic of Texas printed "redbacks." Because of its heavy indebtedness, the Republic of Texas resorted to offering interest-bearing notes to raise funds to retire its indebtedness. In 1840, however, non-interest-bearing notes were issued. Since they were printed with a reddish-colored ink on the back of the note, these notes were called redbacks.

CIVIL WAR STAMPS
During the Civil War, the Texas municipalities of Galveston, Beaumont, Gonzales, Hallettsville, Helena, Independence, and Victoria played a unique role in the postal system: they issued their own postal stamps. Neither the Republic nor the State of Texas issued postage stamps, but during the Civil War, local stamps known as "Confederate postmaster's provisions" were issued by individual municipalities in Texas. These local stamps were not authorized by the Confederacy, but because the Confederate government could not supply its own stamps until October

1861, cities throughout the South produced their own stamps for prepayment postage. The Gonzales stamps are of particular interest because the advertising labels of Coleman & Law Booksellers and Druggists were pressed into service when Law was postmaster of Texas. These stamps are so rare that, in 2015, one ten-cent version sold for $47,500 at auction.

THE GREAT PEARL RUSH

An example of Texas's diversified geographical makeup and resources is the story of the "Great Pearl Rush" of 1909–1911. When very valuable pearls were discovered in Caddo Lake in East Texas, many came with their families to camp on the banks of the lake and search for freshwater mussels containing the pearls. Although this might seem a strange phenomenon for a place like Texas, it was not an isolated incidence, as pearls of various hues have been found in the Concho River as well.

SALT DOMES

Just as Houston's Astrodome changed the playing of certain sports in Texas, and to some degree across the nation, another kind of dome was instrumental in changing the entire economy of Texas, as well as its image. Created eons ago, the geological formations called salt domes, found particularly along the Gulf Coast plains, were the basis for Texas's petroleum industry. The domes trapped and housed the oil and natural gas that gave Texas some of its most productive fields and were responsible for driving the speculators and drillers into oil exploration throughout Texas. One such salt dome produced the fabulous Lucas gusher known as Spindletop, which came in near Beaumont on January 10, 1901. The Spindletop gusher was so powerful that before it was capped, it erupted more than seventy-five thousand barrels a day for six to nine days. Long before Europeans arrived on the oil-rich Texas soil, Indians touted the oil as having medicinal qualities.

TEXAS-SIZE STEAK CHALLENGE

It sounds like a tall Texas tale, but the Big Texan Steak Ranch at Amarillo is the real thing. Known to locals and passers-through alike, the restaurant features a 72-ounce steak for $72, which becomes free if the customer can finish it in under an hour—along with the baked potato, shrimp cocktail, salad, and bread that go with it. The restaurant's founder, R. J. Lee, wanted to prove that Texas cowboys were the biggest eaters and conducted a search for the one who could eat the most. He served the contender one-pound strip steaks until the Texan had eaten four and a half of them (72 ounces). With this as an example, he hit upon the idea of offering the 72-ounce challenge.

According to the restaurant's website, more than 9,500 intrepid souls have successfully taken on the Big Texan challenge since the place opened in 1960. Putting all of those (99 percent male) challengers to shame, in 2015, 120-pound mother of four (and competitive eater) Molly Schuyler ate *three* Big Texans in under twenty minutes. Where there's a will, there's a way . . .

Paris's Eiffel Tower Receives Traditional Texas Topping

We might not be bustin' new sod if we told you that the North Texas city of Paris has its own Eiffel Tower. The 65-foot tower, constructed in 1993, stands next to the Love Civic Center on the corner of Jefferson Road and South Collegiate Drive. What is particularly noteworthy is that in October of 1998, this Texas city's Eiffel Tower was topped by what is, no doubt, one of the state's largest cowboy hats. The red hat is so large—three and a half feet tall and ten feet in diameter—that it took three gallons of "fire-engine" red paint and three hours to paint it. According to the Lamar County Chamber of Commerce, lighting was added in 2012.

Jesus in Cowboy Boots

As if having its own European landmark wasn't enough, in 2016, the Evergreen Cemetery in Paris, Texas, celebrated its 150th anniversary and was designated by the Texas Historical Commission as a state historical landmark. However, the cemetery already had become well known for its unusual grave markers—particularly the one known as "Jesus in cowboy boots." Both the Paris Chamber of Commerce and cemetery staff acknowledge that this statue is one of the city's most visited tourist attractions.

Representatives at Evergreen Cemetery tell us that Willet Babcock, over whose grave the unusual statue stands, was a maker of fine furniture. Mr. Babcock built the first opera house in the city of Paris, and he founded the city's fire department, where he served as chief. Mr. Babcock lived and died in the latter part of the nineteenth century. It is said that he envisioned his Lord Jesus as wearing cowboy boots. He instructed a Mr. Klein, a local stone carver, to make an elaborate monument for his final resting place.

The monument was topped with a statue of Jesus wearing cowboy boots. This monument and other unusual markers have made this huge cemetery so well known that visitors can take guided tours through the more than forty thousand graves.

RATTLESNAKES AND WASPS

Although rattlesnakes and wasps sound more like the residents of an abandoned line shack in the Big Bend country, they are both highly touted by the Sweetwater Chamber of Commerce as valuable attributes of that city—and rightly so!

When one realizes that this friendly but earlier lackluster town started as a store in a dugout on Sweetwater Creek, it is easy to see why the city's world-famous "Rattlesnake Roundup," as well as the home base of the heroic Women Air Force Service Pilots of WWII, better known as WASPs, are touted as the city's claim to fame.

The "World's Largest Rattlesnake Roundup," which is sixty years old, resulted in more than twenty-two tons of western diamondback rattlers being rounded up in 2016. The record length is eighty-one inches. The Jaycees, who sponsor the annual event, reported an attendance of nearly twenty-six thousand in March of 2015 (the latest total available), 83 percent of whom were from out of town. This event, though an unusual claim to fame, has earned bragging rights for this vitally alive Texas city.

"ONE RIOT–ONE RANGER"

Ranking along with "Remember the Alamo," and "Come and take it" of Gonzales fame is the Texas Ranger motto "One Riot–One Ranger." This appropriate motto for the state's oldest law enforcement agency is credited to Ranger captain William J. "Captain Bill" McDonald. According to author Harold Weiss, in his biography of McDonald, Captain Bill arrived in Dallas alone to halt an illegal boxing match that threatened to turn into a riot. When he stepped off the train, a very nervous Dallas mayor asked,

"Where are the rest of the men?" To this, McDonald is supposed to have replied, "Hell, ain't I enough? There ain't but one riot." This motto is visually perpetuated by a bronze statue of a Texas Ranger that greets travelers in the terminal building of Dallas Love Field airport. Its caption reads: "Texas Ranger of 1960 One Riot–One Ranger."

Also credited to the glib and fearless McDonald is a philosophy he verbalized to encourage the men of his company stationed in Amarillo at the turn of the century. He is known for saying, "No man in the wrong can stand up against a fellow that's in the right and keeps on a comin'!" This Ranger died in 1918.

TEXAS'S UNKINDEST INSULT

What most Texans would consider "fightin' words" are attributed to General Phillip H. Sheridan. The general, following the Civil War, was in 1867 made military governor of the Fifth Military District consisting of Louisiana and Texas. On July 30, 1867, after removing several Texas officials from office "because they were detriments to Reconstruction," Sheridan's harsh policies of Reconstruction met with the disapproval of President Andrew Johnson, who removed Sheridan from office as a tyrant. Perhaps influenced by his being stationed in Texas, Sheridan is attributed with making the statement, "If I owned Hell and Texas, I'd live in Hell and rent Texas out!"

HIDDEN SECRETS OF THE
"UGLY OLD GODDESS" OF AUSTIN

Hoisted to the top of the Texas capitol dome in February 1888, the monumental zinc statue known as "the goddess of liberty" remained on the state's symbol of government nearly ninety-eight years. The statue was designed by capitol architect Elijah Myers of Detroit. Its harsh countenance inspired criticism at first, prompting one local newspaper to dub her "Old Lady Goddess," saying that her face "resembles an old woman of eighty." The statue, which was painted white and which held aloft a gilded lone star, stands nearly sixteen feet tall and weighs almost three thousand pounds. In 1986 the statue was taken down for restoration and replaced with an aluminum replica, which led to a surprising discovery.

During the restoration process, a decaying time capsule was discovered inside the five-pointed star originally held by the goddess. Among the remains of spiders, roaches, and winged insects was a copy of *Texas Vorwaerts* (Texas Forward), a German-language newspaper printed in Austin, as well as two Wisconsin newspapers, several business cards, and a "broadside" (advertisement). The finding of the German-language newspaper confirmed a report made in 1946 by the late Edward Schultze of Austin that in 1888 he and his future wife, Emma Wolfe, placed in the star a calling card and a copy of *Texas Vorwaerts,* the newspaper established by Schultze's father in 1883. These long-hidden secrets of the goddess have been preserved for exhibition. The restoration of the statue, which has been on display in the Bullock Museum in Austin, was completed in July of 2017.

Shelby County Courthouse's Trap Door

If we are to believe the Hollywood version of the Old West and the pulp fiction dime novels written about the lives and times of early Texas, the very mention of the words "trap door" struck fear in the hearts of those whose activities skirted the law, particularly those who participated in the outrageous crime of cattle rustling. To those miscreants of early Texas, the words "trap door" conjured up the ghastly image of their standing on a gallows with a hangman's noose around their neck, as they awaited the fatal plunge that would pay their debt to society for their errant ways.

The Shelby County courthouse in Center, Texas, has a built-in trap door that once served as a safety feature rather than something to be feared. In a conversation with county judge Floyd A. "Dock" Watson, we were told that when the 1885 county courthouse was built, an escape hatch was installed near the judge's bench to provide the presiding judge a handy means of escape from irate defendants. The door provided access by way of stairs to the judge's chambers below the bench.

The judge told us that, while there are surely stories of such escapes, he knows of no such incidences personally. Although the trap door had been sealed off for some time, the judge had it reopened, as it was such an interesting attraction in the county courthouse.

"Pecosin'" a Feared Word

Back when law was practically nonexistent in the two-fisted, gun-totin' days of the region around the Pecos River, the term "Pecosin'" meant to dispose of a murder victim by throwing his body in the Pecos. The term had a definite ring of finality to it!

The Jackass Mail

Because road conditions during the days of the Republic of Texas were so poor, with almost no bridges, even stage travel was undesirable. The discovery of gold on the West Coast in 1849 brought about several reasonably reliable stage lines to carry passengers, freight, and mail. One line between San Antonio and El Paso used primarily mules for power and was quickly dubbed "The Jackass Mail."

Rickshaws under Texas Skies

The Texas Centennial in Dallas had one feature that, considering its uncountable sights and sounds that one had to take in, may very well have been forgotten. College boys, as a means of earning tuition as well as keeping in shape, pulled foot-weary fairgoers from street to street and plaza to plaza in rickshaws during the 1936 celebration of our state's one hundredth birthday.

Included in the eclectic music offered by the Texas Centennial was a cowboy singing group, the Sons of the Pioneers.

Leonard Slye, a member of that group, later changed his name to Roy Rogers and married a Uvalde, Texas, songbird by the name of Dale Evans, who got her radio start singing on a Dallas morning variety show, "The Earlybirds." The show was broadcast on radio station WFAA with studios atop the Santa Fe Building on Jackson Street. The "Happy Trails" traveled by this couple are now history in the annals of Western music.

SUPERLATIVES

In a state as amazing as Texas, superlatives are common parlance—we just can't help ourselves. If you're from around here, you understand; if you don't, just come visit a while . . . The following bits of trivia highlight our state's best, worst (yes, we'll admit those, too), first, biggest (plenty of those!), and other singular people, places, things, and events.

First Surgery
In all probability the first recorded surgical operation performed in North America was done in Texas. Spanish explorer Cabaza de Vaca, against his will, gained the respect of Indians as a medicine man and surgeon. He was the first European to practice medicine in the New World. In 1536 he removed an arrow from the chest wall of an Indian, most likely the first recorded surgical operation done in North America. He sewed up the wound and it healed.

First Thanksgiving
Although tradition and history books tell us that the first Thanksgiving was celebrated by English colonists in Massachusetts in 1621, some Texans dispute this. El Paso citizens say they have written proof that the first Thanksgiving in America was celebrated a full twenty-three years earlier in their city. Based on a poem published in 1610, a decade before the *Mayflower* set sail from England, a Thanksgiving feast was held on the banks of the Rio Grande River near what is today El Paso. The poem tells the

story of Spanish settlers, soldiers, and monks who had exhausted their provisions and water while traveling the Mexican desert en route to what is now New Mexico. Nearly dead from hunger and thirst, they came upon the Rio Grande, and with fish and wild game supplied by Indians, they had a feast of thanksgiving and celebrated mass. El Paso citizens claim this celebration by five hundred men, women, and children on April 15, 1598, was the first Thanksgiving held on American soil.

NACOGDOCHES, SITE OF FIRST CHRISTMAS IN TEXAS

One of our state's oldest cities is the East Texas city of Nacogdoches. It brags about having its first European settlement in 1716. Age alone has made this historical city a mother lode of Texas trivia. Not only was Nacogdoches the home of some of Texas's most prominent figures, including Sam Houston, Thomas J. Rusk, and Adolphus Stern, the Texas Revolution also was planned in this place.

The city has one claim to fame that is not well known to most Texans. The state's first Christmas celebration was held in Nacogdoches. Although no Sinterklaas, as he was known to the Dutch, who introduced him to America in New York, was present, the holiday was observed. In 1686 the French explorer LaSalle became ill while visiting Nacogdoches. The Tejas Indians nursed him and cured him. Being a devout Catholic, on Christmas Day, 1686, LaSalle celebrated a Christmas Mass in Nacogdoches. Information provided us by that city tells us that "no reliable documentation has been found which records an earlier Christmas celebration in Texas." This first Christmas in Texas is colorfully celebrated by that city each year.

JOSÉ DE ESCANDÓN

José de Escandón, the Spanish colonizer, was responsible for the first successful settlement along the Rio Grande River between present-day Laredo and Brownsville. He was born at Soto La

Marina in 1700. In 1746 Escandón was commissioned to inspect the country between Tampico and the San Antonio River, then known as "Seno Mejicano." In January 1747 he sent seven divisions into the area. In October he presented a colonization plan. Spanish red tape caused delays, but in June 1748 Escandón was made governor and captain general of Nuevo Santender. In 1749 he began establishing settlements along the Rio Grande, his first two being Camargo and Reynosa. Only two of Escandón's permanent settlements were north of the Rio Grande: Laredo and Dolores. Escandón has been given credit for starting the cattle industry in Texas in 1749 when he brought Mexican Longhorns into the fertile but mosquito-ridden lower delta area along the Rio Grande at the Gulf coast.

ANAQUA
The first site in Texas to be named is thought to be Anaqua, located on the San Antonio River in southern Victoria County. It was described by Cabeza de Vaca as the habitat of the depraved tribe of Anaqua Indians. Carlos de Garza built a ranch and a chapel at the site around 1820. Anglo American settlers came after 1836, and Anaqua continued to be a thriving settlement until 1905, when the Missouri-Pacific Railroad laid tracks five miles to the east and drew away many settlers.

SAN JACINTO FLAG
The restored remains of the original 1835 San Jacinto flag are the oldest artifact in the state capitol of Texas. It hangs behind the Speaker's desk in the House Chamber. The flag features a female figure holding a sword over which is draped a sash or ribbon bearing the slogan "Liberty or Death."

FIRST BAPTIST CHURCH IN TEXAS
The first Baptist church on Texas soil was organized at Washington-on-the-Brazos by Z. N. Morrell in 1837. The adoption and signing

of the Texas Declaration of Independence was done in the black-smith shop of Noah T. Byers, an early settler in whose shop the Congress met temporarily. Byers was an ordained minister in the Baptist church and was given credit for founding a number of Baptist churches as well as other Baptist institutions. He was a member of Texas's first Baptist church at Washington-on-the-Brazos.

OLD NEWS

The *Dallas Morning News* has a history that parallels that of Texas. The A. H. Belo Corporation, publisher of the *Morning News,* goes back to 1842 and the one-page *Galveston News,* before Texas was even a state! The Belo Corp. is the oldest continuously operating business in Texas. George Bannerman Dealy, who founded the *Morning News* in 1885, was a fifteen-year-old English immigrant when he was hired as an office boy at the *Galveston News.* He was full of enthusiasm and energy and quickly moved up in the company. Working tirelessly, Dealy made his way from office boy to business manager and then publisher of the *Dallas Morning News.* It was Dealy who chose the then small settlement of Dallas as a site for the sister publication.

The Legend of the First Bowie Knife

Much has been said about the legendary Bowie knife, but there is enough material on the subject to conclude that the knife was not made by the Alamo hero. While recovering from the "Sandbar duel" in Natchez, Mississippi, Jim Bowie was given the knife by his brother, Rezin Bowie. The details of the making of the knife, which became the hand weapon of choice for many in the Southwest before the advent of the six-shooter, are not fully known. One widely told story, which is said to originate from a Bowie relative, is that Rezin had the knife made to his specifications, which included a large guard between the handle and the blade to prevent the user's fingers from being cut should they slip over the blade during use. It is said that the knife was made in Ayoyelles Parish, Louisiana, from a file in Rezin's blacksmith shop by his blacksmith, Jesse Clifft.

Death by the Rope in Dallas

Before 1914, when the "new" Dallas County jail and Criminal Courts Building was opened, the Dallas County jail was located on Houston Street near where the Union Terminal Station is presently located. Just outside the jail were the gallows, where until the 1920s, when the state assumed the responsibility for executing the state's condemned prisoners, public hangings were carried out. Across the way, where the *Dallas Morning News* building and Ferris Plaza stands, was a wagon yard where spectators gathered to watch the condemned swing. The show stopped when prisoners were moved to the newly constructed jail just down the street at Main and Houston Streets. Hangings were carried out there for the next decade. Although the old gallows were lost to renovation, the death cells can still be seen there.

A history of the Dallas County Sheriff's Office informs us that in 1853 Sheriff Trezevant C. Hawpe presided over Dallas County's first legal hanging. The condemned was a black woman named "Jane." She was convicted of splitting open with an ax the head of a widower named Wisdom, who had hired her to take care of the house and his children.

FIRST FLIGHT

Nearly forty years before the Wright brothers flew their plane at Kitty Hawk in 1903, a Texan flew a fixed-wing powered airplane in Fredericksburg in 1865. Newspaper accounts reveal that Jacob Brodbeck successfully flew an airplane that he had built and that was powered with coil springs. The airplane reached an altitude of tree-top heights before it crashed into a hen house, killing numerous chickens and scaring many children. Brodbeck, a teacher and inventor, came to Texas from Germany in 1846 and lived in Luckenbach.

TEXAS'S FIRST CIVIL RIGHTS MARCH

Texas's first civil rights march was prompted by the shameful actions of the first legislature elected after the 1866 constitutional convention during the days of Reconstruction. The legislature passed a law allowing blacks to testify in court cases only if the case involved other blacks; segregating blacks on public transportation; prohibiting blacks from holding public offices, serving on juries, or voting; and prohibiting blacks from marrying whites. Seeking their civil rights, blacks began to organize chapters of the Loyal Union League. The state's first civil rights march involved one black man in Webberville, near Austin, who in 1868 carried an American flag and a saber and led the town's black voters to the polls to vote in an election on whether to hold another constitutional convention.

FIRST OIL WELL

The first Texas oil well drilled for production was at Melrose, Texas, in Nacogdoches County in 1866. The well was drilled by

Lynis T. Barret, who, unfortunately, couldn't get financial support to continue the venture because potential backers saw only poor market possibilities.

THE FIRST BRIDGE ACROSS THE BRAZOS

Waco's historic suspension bridge over the Brazos River predates New York's famous Brooklyn Bridge and was constructed by the same builder. Until the late 1860s, the only way across the Brazos at Waco was by ferry or by fording the river when the water was low. Captain Shapley Ross had operated a primitive ferry at Waco since 1849, but the Brazos could be treacherous after a rain and was sometimes impassable for days at a time.

Waco business leaders got a charter from the state in 1866 to build a permanent toll bridge over the Brazos. Even with money scarce and interest rates high during Reconstruction, the Waco Bridge Company sold all its stock, and in mid-1868, the company chose John A. Roebling and Son of Trenton, New Jersey, to design and build a new suspension-type bridge. Roebling utilized the same style and technique he later used on the Brooklyn Bridge, which opened in 1883. Civil engineer Thomas M. Griffith, a Roebling employee who had worked with similar bridges, was the actual designer and construction supervisor. Work began in September of 1868. At the time, Waco had no machine shops or any artisans with the skills to build a bridge of this magnitude, and the nearest railroad was one hundred miles away. The woven wire cables and other components were shipped to Galveston by steamer, transferred by rail to Bryan, and then taken by ox wagons on a rutted, dusty road to Waco.

Construction began with the excavation for the footings of the twin double towers that would anchor the span. The towers, which required 2.7 million locally produced bricks to construct, were topped with crenellated ornamentation resembling a medieval castle. Workmen carried wires across the river to form the massive cables that would support the wooden roadway. The span was completed in late December 1869, and the first tolls were collected on January 1, 1870. The $141,000 structure—the first bridge across the Brazos—was dedicated five days later. The main span was wide enough for two stagecoaches to pass each other, and it was 475 feet long.

OLDEST PUBLIC SCHOOL

Austin can lay claim to having the oldest operating public school in Texas. Pease Elementary School was established in 1876, no doubt named for Governor Elisha M. Pease, known as the "education governor." It was Pease who on January 31, 1854, signed the bill setting up the Texas public school system.

TELEPHONES

The first telephones in Texas were installed in 1878 in the home and office of A. H. Belo, publisher of the *Galveston News*. The first long-distance telephone lines in Texas were installed between Houston and Galveston in 1883. The first long-distance direct dialing in Texas was initiated in 1955.

"OLD TIGE"

The City of Dallas's last horse-drawn fire truck was nicknamed "Old Tige" (an abbreviation for tiger) after former mayor William Lewis Cabell, who acquired the nickname while serving as a general in the Confederate army. Purchased in 1884, the truck was a pumper with a steam boiler that supplied the power for pumping the water at up to six hundred gallons per minute. The truck, which was kept in service until 1921, is displayed at the Dallas Firefighters Museum across from Fair Park at 3801 Parry (at Commerce Street).

FIRST AUTO TRIP

The first gasoline-engine automobile in Texas belonged to one-legged Col. E. H. R. "Ned" Green. The automobile was a Phaeton runabout built by the St. Louis Gas Car Co. It had a two-cylinder engine, tiller, and buggy top. The cost to Col. Green for this 1899 model St. Louis was $1,260. This was more than a year's salary for most Texans. Col. Green could well afford the new addition to Texas roads, such as they were in those days, as Col. Green was the son of Hetty Green, the so-called Witch of Wall Street, who was said to be the richest woman in the world. The "horseless carriage" was shipped to Green by its designer, George P. Dorris, who accompanied Green on the first automobile trip in Texas. The trip from Green's home in Terrell, Texas, to Dallas, where Green maintained an apartment, a distance of thirty miles, took the pair five hours in October of 1899. About one hour of that was taken up in the small town of Forney, where an accident occurred.

According to an article in the *Dallas Morning News,* "a farm wagon crowded Green's automobile off the road and into a gully damaging it." This was, no doubt, Texas's first automobile accident. The *News* article also informs us that the accident produced Texas's first automobile repairman as well: "A stop at a blacksmith's shop operated by Henry Reeve, an African-American who operated shops in Forney from the turn of the century until 1920, resulted in Henry being Texas' first auto repairman."

After the accident and subsequent repairs, Green and Dorris left Forney in their St. Louis and proceeded at less than breakneck speeds to Dallas. Green was quoted as saying, "We did not put on full power on country roads. When we struck the asphalt pavement on Main Street [in Dallas], we dared not do so because the thoroughfare was so crowded it would have been dangerous to human life."

The vehicle, built like a Phaeton (buggy), was propelled by a five-horsepower engine that consumed two quarts of gasoline on the trip from Terrell to Dallas. Its tank held three gallons. The importance of this initial run of a gasoline-powered "horseless carriage" was that it introduced to our state a new era of transportation.

THE GREAT STORM OF 1900

The deadliest natural disaster in the United States occurred in Texas: the Great Storm of 1900 in Galveston. By 4 o'clock on the afternoon of September 8, Galveston had suffered pounding rain for four days and was under two feet of standing water. In some areas water was five feet deep. Four hours later, winds peaked at 120 mph and a huge wave of water pushed through the island town, smashing buildings and snapping trees. Six thousand people drowned; some historians put the number at eight thousand. After the storm, the town's population had been reduced by one-third, counting not only the dead and missing but also the seven thousand who moved out of Galveston and never returned.

PUBLIC DEMONSTRATION OF AIRPLANE

The first public demonstration of an airplane in Texas took place February 8, 1910, near Houston when Frenchman Louis Paulhan showed off his French-made fabric-and-wood biplane.

FIRST ALAMO MOVIE

The first movie about the Battle of the Alamo was filmed in 1911 by Parisian filmmaker Gaston Melies. Melies was also the first person to play Colonel William B. Travis in the movie, entitled *The Immortal Alamo*. Melies (apparently not one to shy away from the limelight) cast himself in the part.

THE COOLEST BUILDINGS

In 1922, the Rice Hotel cafeteria became the first building in the Houston area to have air-conditioning. In downtown San Antonio, the historic Milam building was the first high-rise office building in the United States to have air-conditioning installed when it was built in 1928. Although no historic records assert this, it can probably be assumed those locales quickly became the most popular places in Texas to eat and work!

BOWIE COUNTY'S LARGEST BABY

The following physical description of a famous Texan might not be much of a surprise to those of us who watched him for so many years on TV. He was born in DeKalb, Bowie County, Texas, in 1928. He was reported as the largest baby born in Bowie County, weighing fourteen pounds at birth. He was over six feet tall and weighed 200 pounds at age twelve. By the time he became a star football player at Sul Ross University in Alpine, Texas, he was six foot four inches and weighed 275 pounds. This Texas-size Texan was born Bobby Don Blocker but used the Hollywood moniker Dan Blocker when he played "Hoss" Cartwright on NBC's *Bonanza.*

NEW LONDON SCHOOL DISASTER

What has been called the "greatest school disaster in the United States" occurred on the afternoon of March 18, 1937, when 294 students, teachers, and visitors were killed when a natural gas explosion destroyed the New London, Texas, school. A natural gas leak caused natural gas to accumulate under the building. The leak went undetected because, at the time, natural gas was colorless and odorless.

It was this horrendous incident that resulted in today's natural gas having its pungent smell. The disaster prompted legislation requiring natural gas to have an additive to give it an unpleasant odor, making it easily detected. Mr. Carl Huff of Texas Utilities, which owns Lone Star Gas Company, advises that since then his company has used mercaptan to give the fuel its unpleasant odor.

One of the first reporters on the scene in the East Texas town was a temporary relief reporter in the Dallas bureau of the United Press news service. His name was Walter Cronkite. The disaster touched the life of this reporter, who would one day become a household name as a television news celebrity. In his biography, Mr. Cronkite wrote how, upon arrival at the school, the destruction and carnage was apparent, as was the frantic search for loved ones.

TEXAS CITY REMEMBERED

April 16, 1947, was the day the Texas Gulf Coast shook and all of Texas shuddered from the resulting shock waves! For those of us having any personal connection to the Texas City Disaster, it will, as President Roosevelt said of Pearl Harbor, "be a day that lives in infamy."

I was a senior in high school and working part-time at a Dallas funeral home. I recall how management came around to all the employees on duty, especially the embalmers, and alerted us that some of the employees might be called upon to go to Texas City to assist in various ways and to tend to the vast number of casualties that were the result of what became one of the worst disasters in Texas's history.

Pretty impressive on a young adult of my age. Details of that day may have dimmed with time in comparison to the impact the news reports on the radio made that day, so I am glad I can call upon *The New Handbook of Texas* for a description of these events:

At 9:12 a.m. the ship SS Grandecamp, *a French-owned vessel loaded with the highly explosive fertilizer ammonium nitrate, which caught fire early in the morning, exploded while attempts were being made to extinguish the fire. The entire dock area was destroyed, along with the nearby Monsanto Chemical Company and other smaller companies and warehouses. Also destroyed were numerous oil and chemical tanks. Smaller explosions and fires were ignited by flying debris, not only along the industrial area but also throughout the city. A fifteen-foot tidal wave created by the force swept the dock area. The concussion of the explosion, felt as far away as Port Arthur, damaged or destroyed at least 1,000 residences and buildings throughout Texas City.*

The ship SS High Fryer, *in dock for repairs and also carrying ammonium nitrate, had been ignited by the first explosion. It was towed 100 feet from the docks before it exploded,*

sixteen hours later at 1:10 a.m. on April 17. The first explosion had killed 26 Texas City firemen and destroyed all the city's firefighting equipment, including four fire trucks, leaving the city helpless in the wake of the second explosion. Probably the exact number of people killed will never be known. Hundreds of local volunteers began fighting fires and doing rescue work.

Red Cross personnel and volunteers from surrounding cities responded with assistance, until almost four thousand workers were operating. Temporary hospitals, morgues, and shelters were set up.

The ship's anchor monument records 576 persons dead, 398 of whom were identified and 178 were listed as missing. The injured ranged in the thousands. I later saw records that said that more than 3,500 were injured. All records of personnel and payroll at Monsanto Chemical Company were destroyed, and many of the dock workers were itinerants, making identification almost impossible in that area. Firemen, ship's crew, and spectators were killed—and most of the bodies were never recovered. Sixty-three bodies were buried unidentified. The loss of property totaled $67 million.

Litigation over the Texas City disaster was finally settled in 1962 when the U.S. Supreme Court refused to review an appeal court's ruling that the Republic of France, owner of the SS *Grandecamp*, could not be held liable for claims resulting from the explosion.

THE LONGEST NAP

One could hardly write about Texas curiosities without mentioning "Old Rip," the horned frog (or toad, as some call it) that was entombed in the cornerstone of the Eastland County Courthouse in 1897 and found alive *thirty-one* years later, according to published accounts by witnesses. The frog, named for the legendary sleeper Rip Van Winkle of literary fame, was retrieved in February of 1928 when the courthouse was torn down. The frog was alive, although dormant, and after being held a few minutes, he began to respond. An April 14, 1985, article in the *Dallas Morning News* said that "Old Rip" died of pneumonia following a nationwide tour that included a stop at the White House to see President Calvin Coolidge. The elderly frog was laid to rest in a satin-lined casket and put on display in a glass case in the new Eastland County Courthouse.

MOST REPORTED EXTRA-TERRESTRIAL CONTACTS

The much-heralded "Texas hospitality" is evidently taken quite seriously by our celestial neighbors, who interpret literally the phrase "Do drop in anytime." Texas is far ahead of the pack in the United States when it comes to number of meteorite strikes. A study by the Meteoritical Society cataloged 304 through April 2013 (compared to thirty-five states that were in the 0–20 range).

The third-largest meteor crater in the United States is ten miles southwest of Odessa in Ector County. About 500 feet in diameter and 103 feet deep originally, it has filled in and is only about 5–6 feet deep now. Although fragments have been found and analyzed, the main meteor mass has never been discovered.

World's Tallest Column Monument

True to its "bigger and better" boast, Texas has a historical marker taller than the Washington Monument and the Statue of Liberty. It is the San Jacinto Monument, located at the San Jacinto Battleground near Houston. According to the San Jacinto Museum of History, at 567.31 feet, it is the world's tallest column monument.

USS *Texas*

Texas's largest monument is not even made of stone! The US Navy battleship USS *Texas* served the country in two world wars, including as a flagship for Admiral Ernest J. King, Commander of the Atlantic fleet in WWII. At the end of the war, beyond her age of retirement, the "Mighty T" was given to the state of Texas. A commission was established to pay for towing the ship to Texas and providing a permanent berth. The vessel was placed in the Houston Ship Channel near the San Jacinto Monument.

Loving County

Although its name seems inviting enough, Loving County, located on the south plains of West Texas, has always been sparsely populated. Only six farms existed there in 1945, in an area of 647 square miles. Loving County was created from Tom Green County in 1887, and by 1890 its population was a whopping three. By 1900 there were only thirty-two inhabitants. Oil was discovered in 1925, and the population was reported at 195 in 1930. The county was organized in 1893 and was the last Texas county to be organized; the county government was organized in 1931 with Mentone as the county seat. There are no railroads

across the area, and less than four miles of highways lead from the Pecos to Mentone. Its population was 82 according to the 2010 census, making Loving the least populous county not only in Texas but in the entire United States.

LONGEST OF THE LONGHORNS

The longest span of horns in the world is said to belong to a Texas steer by the name of Tejas Tip 2 Tip. The steer supporting this massive hat rack spends his day under the broiling Texas sun in the pastures of a Sugar Land, Texas, ranch, twenty miles southwest of Houston. This survivor of the once-dying breed that developed into a Texas icon is owned by Taylor Cattle Company. As of February 2017, the steer's horns measured 122.75 inches from tip to tip, although the Dewitt County extension agent that took the measurement predicted the eight-year-old steer's horns could continue to grow an inch or two *per side* until age fifteen. Although Guinness World Records has yet to verify this record, Tejas Tip 2 Tip has the previous record holder (also a Texas Longhorn, of course) beat by more than five inches!

SMALLEST STATE PARK

The smallest state park in Texas, at one-tenth acre, is the grave site of Elizabeth Crockett, wife of Alamo hero Davy Crockett. Mrs. Crockett stayed home in Tennessee with her children when Davy came to Texas to fight the Mexicans. Mrs. Crockett came to Texas in 1855 to claim the land granted to Davy for his service at the

Alamo. She lived in Hood County until she died there in 1860. Her grave is in Acton, Texas, near Granbury. It is maintained by the Texas Parks and Wildlife Department.

Glen Rose, Home of Texas's Oldest Unusual Claim to Fame

Glen Rose, county seat of Somervell County, developed around a mill and trading post on the Paluxy River in 1849. Although it was once a health spa, the town enjoys a much older and more durable claim to fame. The first footprints identified as dinosaur tracks were discovered in Wheeler Creek in 1910. Charlie and William Moss found dinosaur tracks in the Paluxy River in 1934. Tracks were chiseled out of the soft limestone and ended up in museums as far away as New York City, as well as in private collections. Preservationists were finally roused by the loss of the county's natural treasure, and the land was eventually incorporated into Dinosaur Valley State Park in 1969. The footprints left by the giant prehistoric lizards that roamed much of Texas qualify as the undisputed oldest claim to fame!

Bibliography

"1865 Gonzales 10c Gold on Black Stamp Makes $47,500 at Robert A Siegel." Justcollecting.com. www.justcollecting.com/miscellania/1865 -gonzales-10c-gold-on-black-stamp-makes-47-500-at-robert-a-siegel (accessed July 14, 2017).

Allinson, Matt. "The Violent History of Trainwreck Publicity." Tycho's Nose. www.tychosnose.com/the-violent-history-of-train-wreck-publicity/.

Alvarez, Elizabeth Cruce, ed. *2016–2017 Texas Almanac.* Austin: Texas State Historical Association, 2015.

Anderson, Greta. *Remarkable Texas Women,* 2nd edition. Guilford, CT: Globe Pequot Press, 2013.

Andrews, Sallie. "City of Grapevine, Texas, Timeline." Grapevine Historical Society. http://grapevinehistory.weebly.com/moments-in-time.html (accessed July 24, 2017).

Bartlett, Donald L., and James B. Steele. *Empire: The Life, Legend, and Madness of Howard Hughes.* New York: W. W. Norton, 1981.

Beaty, William. "What Causes the Strange Glow Known as St. Elmo's Fire?" *Scientific American.* www.scientificamerican.com/article/quotwhat-causes -the-stran/ (accessed July 21, 2017).

Big Texan. www.bigtexan.com (accessed July 10, 2017).

Blue Bell Creameries. www.bluebell.com (accessed July 24, 2017).

Branning, Mark. "Making Peace with the 'Possum." DFW Wildlife Coalition. www.dfwwildlife.org/opossum.html (accessed July 26, 2017).

Broder, David S. "How 'Landslide Lyndon' Earned His Name." *The Washington Post,* March 4, 1990.

Cargo, Kathryn. "Yorktown Steer's Horns Contend for World Record," *Victoria Advocate,* February 18, 2017.

Casa Mañana. www.casamanana.org (accessed July 24, 2017).

Collin Street Bakery. www.collinstreet.com/about_us (accessed July 21, 2017).

Convis, Charles. *Outlaw Tales of Texas: True Stories of the Lone Star State's Most Infamous Crooks, Culprits, and Cutthroats.* Helena, MT: TwoDot Books, 2012.

Cronkite, Walter. *A Reporter's Life.* New York: Knopf, 1996.

Cuero Turkey Fest. www.turkeyfest.org/events (accessed July 8, 2017).

"C.W. Post." *Encyclopaedia Britannica.* www.britannica.com/biography/C-W
-Post (accessed July 8, 2017).

Dallas Morning News, April 14, 1985.

Dallas Times Herald, July 28, 1978.

Darin, Paul, and Tara MacIsaac. "Buried in Time: The Great Wall of Texas
Could Change History." *The Epoch Times,* November 25, 2014. www
.theepochtimes.com/n3/1103905-buried-in-time-the-great-wall-of-texas
-could-change-history/ (accessed July 17, 2017).

"Design of the Lone Star Flag." Texas State Library and Archives Commission. www.tsl.texas.gov/treasures/flagsandmaps/flag-design.html
(accessed July 28, 2017).

"Devil's Rope and Route 66 Museum." Devil's Rope Museum. http://barbwire
museum.com/ (accessed July 8, 2017).

Durso, Joseph. "Bill Shoemaker, 72, Hall of Fame Jockey Who Dominated for
Four Decades, Dies." *The New York Times,* October 13, 2003. www
.nytimes.com/2003/10/13/sports/bill-shoemaker-72-hall-of-fame-jockey
-who-dominated-for-four-decades-dies.html (accessed July 26, 2017).

Fairbank, Katie. "Group Honors Texas Pioneer Woman." *Star-Telegram,*
December 9, 1998.

"Ferguson, James and Miriam (1871–1944; 1875–1961)." *Encyclopedia of the
Great Plains.* http://plainshumanities.unl.edu/encyclopedia/doc/egp
.pg.025 (accessed July 16, 2017).

"First Automobile in Texas, The." Motor Texas. www.motortexas.com/doc
.aspx?id=first-automobile-in-texas.1263 (accessed July 21, 2017).

Forbis, William H. *The Cowboys.* New York: Time-Life Books, 1973.

Fulton, Maurice Garland, ed. *Pat F. Garrett's Authentic Life of Billy the Kid.*
New York: The Macmillan Company, 1927.

Fulton, Maurice G., and Robert Mullin, ed. *History of the Lincoln County War.*
Tucson: University of Arizona Press, 1980.

Gard, Wayne. *Sam Bass.* Lincoln: University of Nebraska Press, 1969.

Garrett, Judith M., and Michael V. Hazel. "Dallas Morning News." *Handbook
of Texas Online.* https://tshaonline.org/handbook/online/articles/eed12
(accessed July 8, 2017).

Greene, A. C. *A Personal Country.* College Station: Texas A&M University
Press, 1979.

"Greer County." Oklahoma Historical Society. www.okhistory.org/publications/
enc/entry.php?entry=GR025 (accessed July 21, 2017).

"Guadalupe Bass." StateSymbolsUSA.org. https://statesymbolsusa.org/symbol
-official-item/texas/state-fish-aquatic-life/guadalupe-bass (accessed July
14, 2017).

Hacker, Margaret Schmidt. "Parker, Cynthia Ann." *Handbook of Texas Online.*
https://tshaonline.org/handbook/online/articles/fpa18 (accessed July 18,
2017).

Haley, J. Evetts. *Charles Goodnight: Cowman and Plainsman.* Norman: University of Oklahoma Press, 1981.

Haythornthwaite, Philip J. *The World War One Source Book.* London: Arms & Armour Press, 1993.

Herda, Lou Ann. "Shelby County Courthouse." TexasEscapes.com. http://texasescapes.com/TRIPS/GreatAmericanLegendTour/ShelbyCounty Texas/ShelbyCountyCourthouse.htm (accessed July 21, 2017).

"Hereford, Texas." TexasEscapes.com. www.texasescapes.com/TOWNS/ HerefordTexas/HerefordTexas.htm (accessed July 8, 2017).

Hitt, Dick. *History of the Dallas County Sheriff's Department.* www.dallascounty .org/department/sheriff/documents/HistoryoftheDallasCountySheriff2 .pdf (accessed July 21, 2017).

Ingham, Donna. *Texas Myths and Legends.* Helena, MT: TwoDot Books, 2017.

Jameson, W. C. *Texas Train Robberies.* Guilford, CT: Lone Star Books, 2017.

"John Neely Bryan, Founder of Dallas." The Robinson Library. www.robinson library.com/america/uslocal/gulf/texas/dallas/bryan.htm (accessed July 13, 2017).

K'nam, Witajče. "Who Are the Wends?" Texas Wendish Heritage, January 1, 2010. www.texaswendish.org (accessed July 24, 2017).

Kanzanjian, Howard, and Chris Enss. *The Cowboy and the Senorita: A Biography of Roy Rogers and Dale Evans.* Helena, MT: TwoDot Books, 2017.

"Kelly Plow Company 1882." The Historical Marker Database. www.hmdb .org/marker.asp?marker=89064 (accessed July 16, 2017).

Kingston, Mike, ed. *1992–93 Texas Almanac.* Houston: Gulf Publishing Company, 1991.

Korotev, Randy L. "Meteorites in the United States." Department of Earth and Planetary Sciences, Washington University in St. Louis. http:// meteorites.wustl.edu/numbers_by_state.htm (accessed July 12, 2017).

Kreneck, Thomas H. "Houston, Samuel." *Handbook of Texas Online.* https:// tshaonline.org/handbook/online/articles/fho73 (accessed July 20, 2017).

Krieger, Margery H. "Quivira." *Handbook of Texas Online.* https://tshaonline .org/handbook/online/articles/bpq02 (accessed July 18, 2017).

Lewis, John E. *The Mammoth Book of the West.* London: Robinson Publishing, 1996.

Long, Christopher. "Jefferson, TX (Marion County)." *Handbook of Texas Online.* https://tshaonline.org/handbook/online/articles/hgj02 (accessed July 28, 2017).

Lynch, Kevin. "Record Holder Profile Video: Lazy J's Bluegrass and the Largest Horn Spread on a Steer (Living)." *Guinness World Records,* September 9, 2015. www.guinnessworldrecords.com/news/2015/9/record-holder -profile-video-lazy-j%E2%80%99s-bluegrass-and-the-largest-horn -spread-on-a-395638.

Manisero, Stef. "Originally Atop the Capitol, Goddess of Liberty Undergoing Restoration." *Spectrum News,* July 12, 2017. spectrumlocalnews.com/tx/austin/news/2017/07/12/originally-atop-the-capitol--goddess-of-liberty-undergoing-restoration.html.

"Marble Falls Began with Adam Rankin Johnson." Marble Falls, Texas. www.marblefallstexas.com/adam-rankin-johnson.html (accessed July 21, 2017).

"March 18, 1937." New London Museum. www.nlsd.net/index2.html (accessed July 21, 2017).

McDowra, Toni. "Evergreen Cemetery Historical Marker Dedication." *eParisExtra,* September 27, 2016. https://eparisextra.com/blog/2016/09/27/evergreen-cemetery-historical-marker-dedication/.

Merriam-Webster's Collegiate Dictionary. Springfield, MA: Merriam-Webster, 2004.

Miller, Edmund Thorton. "Money of the Republic of Texas." *Handbook of Texas Online,* https://tshaonline.org/handbook/online/articles/mpmzv (accessed July 29, 2017).

"Monahans Sandhills State Park." Texas Parks and Wildlife. http://tpwd.texas.gov/state-parks/monahans-sandhills/nature (accessed July 20, 2017).

Morris, John Miller. *El Llano Estacado: Exploration and Imagination on the High Plains of Texas and New Mexico, 1536–1860.* Austin: Texas State Historical Association, 2013.

Mosbergen, Dominique. "120-Pound Molly Schuyler Devours Three 72-Ounce Steaks (Plus Sides) in 20 Minutes, Sets New Record." *The Huffington Post,* April 20, 2015. www.huffingtonpost.com/2015/04/20/molly-schuyler-steak-dinners-record-20-minutes_n_7097946.html (accessed July 8, 2017).

Muir, Andrew Forest. "Rice, William Marsh." Texas State Historical Association. www.explore.rice.edu/explore/a_brief_rice_history.asp (accessed July 18, 2017).

Nash, Robert. *Bloodletters and Badmen: A Narrative Encyclopedia of American Criminals from the Pilgrims to the Present.* New York: M. Evans, 1995.

"Old Tige." The Dallas Firefighters Museum. http://dallasfiremuseum.com/history/old-tige/ (accessed July 8, 2017).

Oxford English Dictionary, 11thedition (revised). New York: Oxford University Press, 2008.

Packard, Dan. "Small Town Hopes for Big Boost from Article." *Amarillo Globe-News,* July 27, 2003.

"Pappy O'Daniel." Texas State Library and Archives Commission. www.tsl.texas.gov/treasures/characters/pappy.html (accessed July 16, 2017).

Paris, Texas/Lamar County Chamber of Commerce. www.paristexas.com/ (accessed July 20, 2017).

Pilcher, Walter F. "Chicken Ranch." *Handbook of Texas Online,* https://tsha online.org/handbook/online/articles/ysc01 (accessed July 19, 2017).

Pittsburg Hot Links. www.pittsburghotlink.com/our-story.html (accessed July 8, 2017).

"Pittsburg: Northeast Texas Rural Heritage Center-Depot Museum and Ezekiel Airship." Texas Forest Trail. http://texasforesttrail.com/plan-your -adventure/historic-sites-and-cities/sites/northeast-texas-rural-heritage -center-depot (accessed July 19, 2017).

"Ringness House History." RingnessHouse.org. http://ringnesshouse.org/ history.html (accessed July 14, 2017).

San Elizario Genealogical and Historical Society. http://sanelizariogenealogy. com/about.htm (accessed July 21, 2017).

"San Jacinto Monument, The." San Jacinto Museum of History. www.sanjacinto -museum.org/About_Us/Media_Kit/ (accessed July 18, 2017).

Sanders, Leonard, and Ronnie C. Tyler. *How Fort Worth Became the Texas-Most City.* Fort Worth, TX: Amon Carter Museum of Western Art, 1973.

Sault, Spring. "Buffalo Gap Historic Village." TexasHillCountry.com. http:// texashillcountry.com/buffalo-gap-historic-village/ (accessed July 17, 2017).

Schreiber, Ronnie. "A Man Who Wears the Texaco Star and the Man Behind the Jingle." The Truth About Cars, November 7, 2014. www.thetruth aboutcars.com/2014/11/man-wears-texaco-star-man-behind-jingle/.

Smith, Justin Harvey. *The Annexation of Texas,* 2nd edition. New York: Macmillan, 1919.

Smokestack Restaurant. www.smokestack.net/history.shtml (accessed July 9, 2017).

"Speaker of the House Fast Facts." United States House of Representatives. http://history.house.gov/Institution/Firsts-Milestones/Speaker-Fast -Facts/ (accessed July 19, 2017).

Stake in the Prairie, Mesquite, Texas, A. Mesquite, TX: Mesquite Historical Committee, 1984.

Stoker, Bram. *Dracula.* Mineola, NY: Dover Publications, 2000.

Stone, Rachel. "How Lindbergh Drive Became Skillman Street." *Advocate,* December 7, 2011. http://lakewood.advocatemag.com/2011/12/07/ how-lindbergh-drive-became-skillman-street/ (accessed July 8, 2017).

"Sunken Grayson Plantation Featured in Austin Exhibit." *Herald Democrat,* May 9, 2014. www.heralddemocrat.com/living/lifestyle/sunken-grayson -plantation-featured-austin-exhibit (accessed July 17, 2017).

Texas Highways. www.texashighways.com (accessed July 10, 2017).

"Texas Military Bases." MilitaryBases.com. https://militarybases.com/texas/ (accessed July 28, 2017).

Tips, Kern. *Football Texas Style: An Illustrated History of the Southwest Conference.* New York: Doubleday, 1964.

"Treaty Oak." Texas A&M Forest Service. http://texasforestservice.tamu.edu/
websites/FamousTreesOfTexas/TreeLayout.aspx?pageid=16153 (accessed
July 8, 2017).

Turner, Martha Anne. *The Yellow Rose of Texas: Her Saga and Her Song.* Austin,
TX: Shoal Creek Publishers, 1976.

Tyler, Ron, and Roy R. Barkley, eds. *The New Handbook of Texas.* Austin: Texas
State Historical Association, 1996.

"Waxahachie's Courthouse Grotesques." TexasEscapes.com. www.texasescapes
.com/TOWNS/Waxahachie/WaxahachieTxEllisCountyCourthouse
Gargoyles.htm (accessed July 20, 2017).

Weiser, Kathy. "The Cadillac Ranch & Quirky Amarillo." Legends of America. www.legendsofamerica.com/tx-cadillacranch.html (accessed July 12,
2017).

Weiss, Harold J. *Yours to Command: The Life and Legend of Texas Ranger Captain
Bill McDonald.* Denton: University of North Texas Press, 2009.

Williamson, William R. "Bowie Knife." *Handbook of Texas Online.* https://tsha
online.org/handbook/online/articles/lnb01 (accessed July 13, 2017).

Woolrich, Willis R. "Air-Conditioning." *Handbook of Texas Online.* https://
tshaonline.org/handbook/online/articles/cmarp (accessed July 29, 2017).

"World's Largest Rattlesnake Roundup." Sweetwater Jaycees. www.rattlesnake
roundup.net/ (accessed July 8, 2017).

WPA Dallas Guide and History, The. Dallas: University of North Texas Press,
1993.

Yoakum, Henderson K. *History of Texas: From Its First Settlement in 1685 to Its
Annexation to the United States in 1846.* New York: Redfield, 1856.

Young, Charles H. *Grapevine Area History.* Grapevine, TX: Grapevine Historical Society, 1979.

About the Authors

The late **Bill Cannon** was a Texas native who presented daily trivia on Dallas's KAAM radio station. His other books include *Texas, Land of Legend and Lore*; *Tales from Toadsuck, Texas*; *Treasury of Texas Sayings*; and *Treasury of Texas Humor*.

Courtney Oppel, also a native Texan, is a freelance writer and editor for Rowman & Littlefield and has worked for Pearson Education, Bangtail Press, and About.com. She lives with her husband and two children in Helena, Montana.